THE SOUL OF
THE ORGANIZATION
HOW TO IGNITE EMPLOYEE ENGAGEMENT
AND PRODUCTIVITY

David B. Zenoff

Apress®

ISBN-13 (pbk): 978-1-4302-4965-8
ISBN-13 (electronic): 978-1-4302-4966-5

President and Publisher: Paul Manning
Acquisitions Editor: Morgan Ertel
Editorial Board: Steve Anglin, Mark Beckner, Ewan Buckingham, Gary Cornell, Louise Corrigan, Morgan Ertel, Jonathan Gennick, Jonathan Hassell, Robert Hutchinson, Michelle Lowman, James Markham, Matthew Moodie, Jeff Olson, Jeffrey Pepper, Douglas Pundick, Ben Renow-Clarke, Dominic Shakeshaft, Gwenan Spearing, Matt Wade, Tom Welsh
Coordinating Editor: Rita Fernando
Copy Editor: Ann Dickson
Compositor: Bytheway Publishing Services
Indexer: SPi Global
Cover Designer: Anna Ishchenko

Distributed to the book trade worldwide by Springer Science+Business Media New York, 233 Spring Street, 6th Floor, New York, NY 10013. Phone 1-800-SPRINGER, fax (201) 348-4505, e-mail orders-ny@springer-sbm.com, or visit www.springeronline.com. Apress Media, LLC is a California LLC and the sole member (owner) is Springer Science + Business Media Finance Inc (SSBM Finance Inc). SSBM Finance Inc is a Delaware corporation.

For information on translations, please e-mail rights@apress.com, or visit www.apress.com.

Apress and friends of ED books may be purchased in bulk for academic, corporate, or promotional use. eBook versions and licenses are also available for most titles. For more information, reference our Special Bulk Sales–eBook Licensing web page at www.apress.com/bulk-sales.

Any source code or other supplementary materials referenced by the author in this text is available to readers at www.apress.com. For detailed information about how to locate your book's source code, go to www.apress.com/source-code/.

Advance Praise for

The Soul of the Organization

"While metrics can tell us much about an organization's performance, David Zenoff's book captures something that is as elusive as it is critical—the organization's soul, which transcends the individual interests of its workers and lets them believe they, together, are part of something meaningful and important. Few assets have a more enduring value, and Zenoff has skillfully analyzed it."

—The Rev. John I. Jenkins, C.S.C.

President

University of Notre Dame

"In my 45 years in business, I have learned, as David Zenoff illustrates so well in this book, that positive employee engagement, motivation, and recognition for a job well done at all levels in any organization, profit or not-for-profit, is the key to long-term success. It's what's in employees' hearts, not just their heads, that produces results. In hiring people, I don't care how much they know until I know how much they care. *The Soul of the Organization* provides real-world examples and a clear blueprint for how organizations can create or fortify their souls to inspire employee engagement and produce superior results."

—Dick Kovacevich

Former Chairman and Chief Executive Officer

Wells Fargo & Company

"David Zenoff knows what makes successful organizations work. He provides a very promising new way for leaders to seek high levels of employee engagement and satisfaction and reap the benefits of employees' discretionary effort on behalf of their organization. His insights about successful organizations' souls ought to help many firms and non-profit organizations up their performance significantly."

—Ram Charan

Co-author of

Execution: The Discipline of Getting Things Done

"David Zenoff challenges leaders to examine carefully their organization's soul, an often overlooked yet critical dimension of organizational success. By drawing on engaging case studies from his rich professional experience, Zenoff offers a compelling and accessible framework that leaders can adapt to their institutions. For anyone who cares about building an organizational culture that combines excellence and impact with engagement and care, Zenoff provides a valuable contribution to the literature."

— James E. Canales

President and Chief Executive Officer

The James Irvine Foundation

"David does an outstanding job of identifying and exploring an organization's soul. This approach clearly creates a more holistic lens into an organization's mission and values. He is able to provoke thought around core beliefs and how they determine an organization's culture and key strategies. A thoughtful and inspiring read for leaders."

—Michael J. Angelakis

Vice Chairman and Chief Financial Officer

Comcast Corporation

"Dr. Zenoff's book both inspires and instructs on how great business is done. *The Soul of the Organization* is an important book for the business community to read."

—Laura J. Alber

President and Chief Executive Officer

Williams-Sonoma, Inc.

"David Zenoff offers a wise and well-reasoned argument for tapping into soul and higher meaning as the powerful and enduring motivating elements of organizational culture."

—Chris Brahm

Partner and Director

Bain & Company

"David Zenoff first worked with me as a management consultant at Glaxo and later at Roche. His ability to understand complex organizations and advise leaders on how to resolve barriers to higher performance and build high-performing organizations, where employees find great satisfaction from their work and are proud to be associated with the company, is impressive. His contributions to Roche were responsible for significant sales and profit improvements. I can therefore highly recommend *The Soul of the Organization*."

—Dr. Franz B. Humer

Chairman and former Chief Executive Officer

Roche

"The Soul of the Organization helps to explain those organizations that have cracked the code on how to ignite and sustain employee engagement beyond the conventional vision, mission, and values that almost all organizations now have. David's concept of the organization's soul is a very good way of understanding the special factors in an organization that unleash employees' passion, shared positive spirit, and hope for the collective future, all of which can help organizations attract and retain committed workforces, build strong reputations, and ultimately continue for long periods of time. In addition, his case studies are very powerful in helping to illustrate the existence and particular qualities of an organization's soul. This book is an important contribution to management thinking about successful organizations, and I commend it to you as an essential read."

—Richard Gillingwater

Dean

Cass Business School, University of London

"At a time when corporate and government misdeeds have badly dented the world economy, and the growing demonstrations against Wall Street greed reflect deep cynicism about corporate life, David Zenoff has convincingly made the case to be hopeful. He shows that even financial firms can have a soul, genuine care for solving human problems, and matching practices to manifest their passions. Anyone who wants their hope restored for organizations should read this inspiring book, learning from his corporate and non-profit examples about what is possible and how to attain it."

—Allan R. Cohen

Edward A. Madden Distinguished Professor of Global Leadership

Babson College

Co-author of *Influencing Up*

"Rich in experience, Dr. Zenoff has cultivated unique and powerful insights from his 40-plus years' involvement as an advisor to both leading and evolving companies. Boards, senior leaders, and managers at all levels will gain valuable professional lessons and know-how from reading this book as they seek to build lasting, successful, and culturally rich organizations."

—Julie Howard

President and Chief Executive Officer

Navigant Consulting, Inc.

"David Zenoff combines the experience, wisdom, and insight of his career to illuminate the soul of successful organizations. A powerful gift. He inspires through affirmation and clarity in equal doses, balancing humanity and metrics adeptly. His invitation for us to see our work through a new lens gives us a generative tool for assessing and improving our schools. Thank you, David!"

—Coreen R. Hester

Head of School

The American School in London

Pattie Dunn Jahnke (1953-2011)

To my long-time dear friend, whose concerns for others, keen insights, dedication to what is right, ability to enjoy life's humor and irony, and enormous personal courage lifted the bar, inspired, instructed, empowered, and gave hope to all of us who were somehow touched by her persona and acts. She was a star corporate leader, role model, philanthropist, family member, and friend.

Contents

About the Author

David B. Zenoff has advised more than 90 major companies and not-for-profit organizations in 31 countries over his 45-year career. His consultation work, which principally serves senior executives and boards of directors, focuses on organizational development, renewal, major changes, and strategy formulation.

He has served on the boards of directors of three public U.S. companies and has been a member and chair of the board of directors of a San Francisco not-for-profit organization.

He received his Bachelor of Arts degree from Stanford University and both his Master of Business Administration and Doctor of Business Administration degrees from Harvard Business School.

Earlier in his career, Dr. Zenoff taught at the Stanford Graduate School of Business, Columbia Graduate School of Business, and Institut pour l'Etude des Methodes de Direction de l'Enterprise (now the International Institute for Management Development) in Switzerland.

This is his ninth book. An earlier book, *International Financial Management* (Prentice-Hall, 1969), which he co-authored with Jack Zwick, won a national book award.

He divides his time between San Francisco and La Barboleuse, Switzerland. He is a devoted husband, father, and grandfather; an avid hiker; a Stanford sports fan; and a former marathon runner.

Acknowledgments

Conceptualizing this book took many years and included many twists and turns. I continuously sought greater clarity about what high-performing organizations possessed that was so attractive to their workforces and captured employees' commitment. Did the concept of an organization possessing a soul make sense, and what does an organization's soul consist of? Should the focus of this book be about organizational soul or about providing hope for employees of organizations, since both are of vital interest to me? Indeed, as I explored relevant topics, my working title evolved from Hope and the Corporate Soul to Hope and the Organization Soul to Hope for the Organization Soul to The Soul of the Organization. Likewise, my ideas about the intended audience for the book evolved over time from North American business leaders to North American organizational leaders to organizational leaders anywhere in the world to anyone who works in any organization and wants to better understand and contribute to employees' and their own satisfaction, meaning, and commitment to their organization and its overall success.

The evolution of my intentions for the book's purpose, content, and audience was significantly helped along the way by the wise counsel, feedback, and encouragement of several friends and relatives, as well as by the goodwill and interest of many individuals working in organizations with rich souls, who granted me access and explanations about their organizations. Without all of these forms of support, I could not have written this book or enjoyed every step of the journey: conceptualizing, researching, and writing. My abundant gratitude, respect, and affection to each of you supporters.

For wise counsel, ideas, feedback, and encouragement: Liz Levy Ward was a very smart, imaginative, and positive-minded conversation partner in all facets of creating the vision for the book and pursuing its development, as well as a talented and thoughtful editor. Professor Allan R. Cohen generously and candidly shared his ideas and experiences as an author of many respected organizational development books, and he provided vital feedback after reading an early draft. Curt Berrien, George Lula, and Julie Howard read an early draft of the manuscript and provided invaluable suggestions and feedback. My agent, Sam Fleishman, made insightful suggestions about the book's potential, audience, and purpose, and he encouraged me to include my relevant interpretations of Apple and Steve Jobs's greatness. My talented and positive-spirited Apress editor, Morgan Ertel, who understood from the outset the vision for this book, continually encouraged me to express the passion I feel toward the topic, and sensitively edited the manuscript to enhance its readability.

Several friends provided key counsel, introductions, and encouragement for me including Catherine Armsden, Tom Davenport, Bill Goodyear, Walter Green, and Sam Hayes. And other friends expressed their interest in the book's concepts and my progress and offered ample encouragement along the way: Rick Berthold, Marilyn Campbell, Jay Cuetera, Jay Fudemberg, Patricia Horgan, Al Martin, and Toru Nakamura. Thank you.

My access to the relevant information, remembrances, and explanations about the 11 organizations that are the book's principal examples of organizational soul, plus helpful information and insights about Apple, were generously provided by Sherilyn Adams, Laura Alber, Barbara Babcock, Tom Babcock, Mary Taylor Behrens, Garrett Bouton, Lori Bush, Pat Connolly, Paul Critchlow, Lynn Downey, Michael Giles, Elon Ginzburg, Harry Hagey, Patti Hughes, Robert Haas, Bill Jahnke, Pattie Dunn Jahnke, Emily Janowsky, Rev. John I. Jenkins, Blake Jorgensen, Debbie Jorgensen, Richard Kovacevich, Marilyn Lacey, Howard Lester, Kathie Lowry, John L. Martin, Sharon McCollam, Allen Olivo, Howard Pearson, Amnon Rodan, Mary Ann Scofield, Phil Schlein, Greg Serrurier, Walter S. Schwartz, Jeff Wachtel, and Bill Waters. Each person associated with the 11 principal example organizations granted me one or more interviews and also reviewed sections of the manuscript about their organization for accuracy and completeness. Thank you for your interest, confidence, courtesy, and availability.

Eleven individuals whom I know professionally as clients, colleagues, volunteers, and/or friends were generous in providing endorsements for the book and me after having reviewed a late-stage manuscript draft: Laura Alber, Michael Angelakis, Chris Brahm, Jim Canales, Ram Charan, Allan R. Cohen, Coreen Hester, Julie Howard, Franz Humer, Rev. John I Jenkins, and Richard Kovacevich. Thank you for your interest, respect, trust, courtesy, and time. I am honored by your confidence.

Until late in the manuscript drafting process, I was reliant on three flexible and talented typists, who good-naturedly worked on the latest versions of chapters, somehow discerning what I meant by cross outs and handwritten revisions: Michael Burdick, Mary Dang, and Genevieve Watts. Thank you for your diligence, goodwill, availability, and dedication.

My family members showed considerable interest in my book project from the beginning and expressed wholehearted encouragement along the way. My children—Andrew, Fay, and Alexandra—were enthusiastic and patient listeners to my reports of progress in field research and writing. Alexandra was kind enough to read a late-stage manuscript draft and to diplomatically offer feedback. Likewise, my sister Vicki, my sister- and brother-in-law Laurie and Jonathan, and my former son-in-law Elon encouraged me to push ahead when I was distracted by my day job or slow in creating first drafts of new chapters. In early stages, there was much good-natured family humor about my taking a full year to evolve the working title from Hope and the Organization Soul to Hope for the Organization Soul—as my only visible sign of progress in year one! Thank you for your loving support.

At every stage in authoring this book (conceptualization, research, analysis, writing, and editing), my wife, Janet, was at my side, pitching in with ideas, feedback, questions, typing, proofreading, patient listening and interest, nonstop encouragement, respect, courtesy, and celebration of milestones. This book project is thus a good reflection of our life together, with our support for each other's endeavors. Thank you.

Notwithstanding the many persons noted above who generously contributed to this book, I alone bear responsibility for any inaccuracies or errors.

Introduction

How can it be that vast numbers of employees across industries are demoralized, disengaged, dissatisfied, disrespected, and worn out, while concurrently organization executives are trying to figure out how to motivate their employees to give more of themselves and assume greater responsibility and accountability, control turnover, build greater cooperation and teamwork, while, cutting expenses for the umpteenth time? Why is it that only a relatively small number of successful businesses and not-for-profit organizations have employees who are happy, engaged, committed, proud of their employers and their own work-related contributions, and highly productive year after year? Very few organizations have cracked the code on how to ignite and sustain employee engagement while boosting individual and overall organization productivity. So the question must be asked: What "something special" do high-performing organizations possess that fosters not just admirable and positive work environments but also sustains high levels of overall organizational performance?

Over my long my career, which has included time spent as an academic, a management consultant, a company board member, and a volunteer for not-for-profit organizations, I have had the fortunate experience of observing and helping a wide variety of organizations at work in more than 30 countries. Whenever I have encountered organizations that seemed to exhibit that something special, I sought to understand the "magic" elements in those organizations' leadership, cultures, and management practices that produced such unusually positive results. For a while, I believed that these organizations' magic consisted principally of formulating an organizational vision, mission statement, and set of core values to clarify and motivate executives and employees throughout the organization. And, indeed, for several organizations, my role as consultant was to guide executive groups and facilitate their development of a vision, mission, and set of values for their organization.

Without doubt, I have seen the positive potential and power that the formulation process and conclusions can have.

But, in recent years, I have come to believe that the relatively few organizations that perform so well over time and possess that something special likely offer more than vision, mission, and values to deeply touch their employees' hearts and minds. As this book will exemplify and explain, I believe these organizations' something special comprises five elements that, taken together, form a rich organizational soul with the power to deeply inspire, guide, motivate, engage, and satisfy employees for a long period of time.

To develop greater understanding of organizations that are able to engage employees at such a deep level, I drew upon what I knew about more than 100 business, not-for-profit, and public sector organizations with which I had familiarity. Among those organizations with something special, I sought significant relevant causality and commonalities that could be understood and replicated.

In the case of not-for-profit organizations, it was readily apparent that their *causes* were great sources of meaning, inspiration, satisfaction, and motivation to their staff, volunteers, and boards of directors. People associated with not-for-profits were often strongly touched by the targeted group their organizations were trying to help, the problems in the world they were trying to solve, and what benefits they provided to those in need. Part of their motivation can be summed up in the mission statements such organizations adhere to, such as National Geographic Society ("Inspire People to Care About the Planet"); M.D. Anderson Cancer Center ("Eliminate Cancer in Texas, the Nation, and the World"); and Room to Read[1] ("World Change Starts with Educated Children").

But what about business enterprises? Could employees' involvement in making, distributing, and selling products and services to earn profits and serve (often unknown) shareholders "turn them on" in the workplace? How should companies whose employees were very moved by and committed to their company's notably strong value systems be understood in this regard? Hewlett-Packard's "HP Way," which encompassed the founders' philosophies about the workings and relationships among the company, its employees, and society as well as Johnson & Johnson's "Credo," a page-long set of principles intended to guide the firm's priorities and dedication, were not "causes" such as those that drive not-for-profit organizations' employees. Yet, employees of Johnson & Johnson and Hewlett-Packard (both of which had been longtime,

---

[1] A not-for-profit that builds schools and libraries for children in Asia. It has helped more than 100,000 children gain access to books.

very successful[2] businesses) were known to have been turned on for decades by the cultures and values of their organizations.[3] Similarly, the oft-praised Nordstrom employees' zeal for providing outstanding customer service and satisfaction is a reflection of being turned on by the company's core values and principal goals related to serving others.

In this regard, former IBM chairman Thomas Watson, Jr.'s observation is instructive and compelling: "The basic philosophy, spirit, and drive of an organization have far more to do with its relative achievements than do technological or economic resources, organization structure, innovation, and timing. All these things weigh heavily in success. But they are, I think, transcended by how strongly the people in the organization believe its basic precepts and how faithfully they carry them out."[4]

How can the something special of Apple be explained? How much of its organizational turn-on is the result of genius Steve Jobs's philosophy, persona, vision, strategy, zeal, innovativeness, imagination, and brilliance in conceptualizing the company's evolution over many years?[5] How important to current Apple employees are stories of Steve Jobs and his early struggles to found and build the company? Or Apple's early "David and Goliath" battle with IBM (and the use of the "Think Different" slogan to catch attention and summarize Apple's distinctiveness)? Or Steve Jobs's return to Apple? Or the recent dynamic growth and top-in-the-world valuation of Apple as a present-day consumer products company? How much of Apple's turn-on resulted from its causes, its culture, its philosophies, and its journey?

---

[2] From its 1938 founding, HP grew nearly 20 percent a year for 50 years without a loss. "Architects of the Information Age," *Business Week* (March 29, 2004): 22. Between 2005 and 2010,the company produced 35-percent annual growth in earnings per share. For a long time, J & J, the world's second largest manufacturer of health-care products in 2011, with more than $60 billion in revenues and $13 billion in profits, was considered to be among the best-managed large U.S. companies.

[3] These results are aligned with what Richard Barrett, an expert on values-based leadership, found: "Our experience in mapping the values of more than 1,000 private and public sector institutions over the past ten years allows us to state categorically that values-driven organizations are the most successful organizations on the planet." Source: Richard Barrett, "Liberating the Corporate Soul" (monograph; February 2009).

[4] Thomas Watson, Jr., *A Business and Its Beliefs*, (McGraw-Hill: 1963, p. 5).

[5] "The company was so built around his sense of design and innovation, it was lost when he wasn't there," said Heidi Roizen, vice president of Apple in 1996. "Innovation Entrepreneurs," *Fortune* (November 15, 2004): 190. Note: Examples and discussion of Apple throughout this book are based on understandings the author gleaned from conversations with a former Apple board member and a former Apple executive and from several articles and two recent books: Walter Isaacson, *Steve Jobs*, (Simon & Schuster, 2011), and Adam Lashinsky, *Inside Apple*, (Business Plus, 2012).

If it is true that Steve Jobs, the founder, leader, and visionary of the company, has been a key reason that Apple is so turned on as an organization and its employees so engaged, was that also true at HP and other turned-on firms that had great founders and leaders? Was the story of HP's founding, set in a Palo Alto garage[6] amid fruit orchards with $538 in startup capital, an important source of meaning, inspiration, satisfaction, and proud identity for thousands of HP employees over the years? How important is it that Hewlett and Packard built the company over the years with originality, courage, and great integrity?

In the cases cited thus far, notwithstanding their specific something special ingredients, each company very strongly touched the emotions of their employees, aroused their passions, appealed strongly to their sensibilities, and compellingly engaged them.[7] Their employees responded by becoming committed and energized in their workplace. They identified with the organization with pride and loyalty; they cared about their contributions and the organization's results; they offered their wit, energy, and goodwill; and they derived inspiration, satisfaction, self-pride, and meaning[8] from their employment.

These organizations possessed in common some kind of life force, "deep intelligence,"[9] "intensity of feeling and knowing,"[10] and a distinctive organizational spirit. In spiritual, psychological, and historical treatises, these characterizations have been used to describe a soul.

---

[6] The Palo Alto garage now bears a plaque that reads "Birthplace of 'Silicon Valley.'"

[7] "Engaged employees were twice as likely to be high performers as those who are less engaged ... when employees are engaged, their organization enjoys higher productivity, has lower turnover, and is more likely to attract top talent." Source: Watson Wyatt; quoted and discussed in Neal E. Chalofsky, *Meaningful Workplaces*, (Jossey-Bass, 2010, p. 132).

[8] "What we learned from thousands of ... middle-income Americans ... often experience more stress from feeling they are wasting their lives doing meaningless work ... they hunger to serve the common good and to contribute something with their talents and energies, yet find that their actual work gives them little opportunity to do so. They often turn to demands for more money as a compensation for a life that otherwise feels frustrating and empty ... we uncovered ... the desire to have meaningful work, work that people believe would contribute to some higher purpose than self-advancement." Michael Lerner, *The Politics of Meaning*, (Perseus Books, 1997, pp. 5, 6). "Employees who find meaning in their work are more satisfied, more engaged and, in turn, more productive. They work harder, smarter, more passionately and creatively. They learn and adapt. They are more connected to customer needs. And, they stick around." Dave Ulrich and Wendy Ulrich, *The Why of Work*, (McGraw-Hill, 2010, p. 3).

[9] Thomas Moore, *Care of the Soul*, (Harper Perennial, 1992, p. 229).

[10] Jacob Needleman, *American Soul*, (Jeremy P. Tarcher/Putnam, 2002, p. 333).

As noted earlier, organizations that possess a strong soul (as it will be defined, explained, and exemplified in this book) seem to go beyond even those organizations that offer their employees a vision of their future and/or a mission and/or a set of core values. Organizations with the five elements that I believe comprise a strong soul appeared to possess additional and deeper sources of vitality and meaning that unleash employee passion, engagement, and satisfaction. Engagement is key.

The Power of Employee Engagement

Employee engagement, as numerous research studies have shown, is both a rare and powerful force. According to the *Gallup Management Journal's* "Employee Engagement Index," only 29 percent of employees are actively engaged in their jobs; 54 percent are not engaged; and 17 percent are actively disengaged.[11] According to the same study, "engaged workers produce more money for the company and create emotional engagement and loyal customers. They stay with the organization longer and are more committed to quality and growth than are the other two groups of not-engaged and actively disengaged workers."

The difference between engaged and disengaged employees is also documented in the *2011 Blessing White Employee Global Report*:

- Engaged employees plan to stay at an organization because of *what they give*; the disengaged stay because of what they get.

- Engaged employees have a line of sight to their own future and to the organization's purpose and goals. They are enthused and in gear, using their talents and discretionary effort to make a difference in their employer's drive for sustainable success.

The return on investment of employee engagement has been documented in research by Tower Watson, Gallup, Manpower, and SHRM. These studies link high engagement to discretionary effort, innovation, and customer loyalty. Among the results:

- Hewitt Associates: High-engagement firms had total shareholder returns that were 19 percent higher than average

---

[11] Source: "Leadership Advantage," www.leadershipadvantage.com/powerofengagement.html.

in 2009. In low-engagement organizations, total shareholder returns were 44 percent below average.[12]

- Gallup: "Organizations with comparatively high proportions of engaged employees were much less likely than the rest to see a decline in 2008 EPS, the year after the recession officially began."[13]

- Wharton Business School: An analysis of the "Best Companies to Work For in America" indicated that "high levels of employee satisfaction generate superior long-horizon returns."[14]

Recognizing what organizational soul is about and how it can be developed, nourished, and used to best serve an organization and its employees' needs is the purpose and essence of this book. Ensuing chapters will show the following:

1. Some organizations can be seen to have strong souls (even if no one in the organization calls it that) (Chapters 2 and 3).

2. Souls are comprised of five elements that individually and collectively have great power and benefit (Chapter 4).

3. A strong organizational soul is the something special that offers employees meaning, inspiration, and pride in their workplace, and it can unleash employees' passion, goodwill, shared positive spirit, and energy on behalf of the organization as well as hope for their individual and collective future. Organizations with strong souls can perform very well vis-à-vis achieving their objectives, effectively serving their clients, attracting a committed workforce, building strong reputations, and continuing as such for long periods of time (Chapter 4).

4. Organizations can nourish and protect their souls so that they have remarkable "staying power" (Chapter 5).

5. But souls can be weakened or destroyed by neglect, certain organizational circumstances, or by deliberate action (Chapter 6).

---

[12] Hewitt Associates, "Percent of Organizations with Falling Engagement Scores Triples in Two Years," (press release; July 29, 2010).

[13] Gallup Consulting, *State of the American Workforce: 2008–2010.*

[14] Wharton School, University of Pennsylvania, June 26, 2010.

6. New organizations can deliberately create their soul, and more mature organizations can find, resurrect, and/or build their soul anew (Chapters 7 and 8).

▧ **Note**　The book relies heavily on current and recent examples of companies, not-for-profit organizations, and a public sector enterprise that have strong and evident souls. The example organizations are all very successful in pursuing their missions and objectives and are among the most respected in their fields nationally. I had access to each organization through relationships with one or more of its executives, in most cases because of my professional or volunteer involvement. The examples are meant to clarify my ideas and assertions for the reader, to prompt further thought, and to guide organizations or individuals within organizations who want to perpetuate, strengthen, create, or revive their organization's soul. However, there is no way to prove that the example organizations perform well because of their souls; and this book is not intended as a comprehensive study of organizations' souls. That many of the examples are from the San Francisco Bay Area, and all of them are from the U.S. does not per se limit the applicability of the organization soul framework geographically or in nationality terms. As the book will reveal, there are great differences in the specific elements of soul from one organization to the next, even within industries (for example, the book describes the very different souls of BGI and Dodge & Cox, both investment managers, and of Notre Dame and Stanford, both universities). Different regional and national cultures will tend to place more importance on certain elements of soul because of differences in what excites individuals' passions and intellects. But, the soul framework and concepts presented in this book remain valid and of potential use to organizations, employees, leaders, and managers everywhere.

Examples of Ingredients in Not-for-Profit Organizations' Souls

The findings begin with four examples of not-for-profit organizations—Larkin Street Youth Services, Sisters of Mercy, University of Notre Dame, and Stanford University—as well as one example of a public sector enterprise—San Francisco International Airport—whose souls are strong.

Larkin Street Youth Services

"I am homeless because my dad died and my mother is homeless. I've been on the streets for nine years." So explained Chris one evening last year to a youth counselor at Larkin Street Youth Services, a San Francisco not-for-profit that cares for homeless and runaway youth, helping many young people get off the streets for good. Thanks to all of those years on the streets, Chris was depressed and often scared, but he lacked the skills to cope with the world beyond the streets, and he was without a lifeline or source of hope.

In San Francisco, almost 6,000 such youth each year live in various parks and out-of-the-way places, seeking to survive. Typical of the path taken annually by hundreds of such homeless youth, Chris followed several buddies to Haight Ashbury and into a small storefront outreach center named Larkin Street. At the center, Chris received water, some snacks, clean socks, and an explanation of San Francisco's services for needy youth. As with most youth, it took Chris several days and several follow-up visits to the small outreach storefront to develop enough trust in the agency to consider exploring one or more of the suggested youth programs and facilities. Ultimately, Chris asked to spend the night at the Lark Inn, an emergency shelter center housing forty 18- to 24-year-old homeless men and women.

At Lark Inn, Chris had a warm dinner, a clean bed, a safe environment, and a locker for his belongings. The next morning, he and the other residents had breakfast with a few Larkin Street staff. Over the ensuing days, Chris reapplied for continued emergency shelter at the Lark Inn. Through casual conversations he had there, Chris sensed that most of the inhabitants were drug- or alcohol-addicted. Some had been on the streets for several years, others for only a week. Some were from impoverished families, like his own, who were unable to care for their children. Most had been sexually, physically, and/or psychologically abused by adults. Some were gay or lesbian and had been treated as "unacceptable" by their families and schoolmates. Psychologically, all were badly wounded from their childhood experiences. Most considered street life to be bleak and harsh. Yet, somehow, they deemed it safer than what they had left behind and harbored dreams about their lives, without any clarity about how to pursue them.

Larkin Street began 27 years ago. A group of concerned San Franciscans saw a need in their neighborhood that no one else was filling—the need to provide shelter to homeless youth, many of whom had migrated to San Francisco during the "Summer of Love" era. The organization that began by offering modest shelter to these youth evolved over time, gradually serving more needy youth with support services in addition to shelter. Eventually, Lark Inn was able to welcome *all* youth, no matter in what shape they presented themselves. The only requirements for emergency shelter were to follow the house rules, show respect for others and their belongings, and within 21 days of having begun residence there, with a Larkin Street case manager's help, create a personal development plan for leaving the streets.

Today, Larkin Street annually touches the lives of about 3,400 homeless and marginally housed youth in San Francisco through emergency, transitional, and longer-term housing; case management; access to health care; GED tutoring; psychological and substance abuse counseling; college admission counseling and support; job readiness training; career counseling; job placement support;

and, a stable, positive, and uplifting environment. During its 27 years in existence, Larkin Street has reached more than 70,000 homeless and at-risk youth; and its dedicated staff of 160, motivated by the organization's worthy mission and by its belief in never giving up on a youth who comes into the program, works with tireless dedication. Every member of Larkin Street's carefully recruited board of directors, which includes over 25 of the top business, professional, and community leaders in the Bay Area, is passionate about the organization's mission. All the members are willing to roll up their sleeves and give generously of their time and resources. And their results have been impressive: 76 percent of the youth who participate in the full continuum of Larkin Street services will exit street life for good, garnering national acclaim for the organization's effectiveness.

Larkin Street's community of passionate and skilled staff, board members, volunteers, and financial supporters have been inspired, guided, and galvanized by seven core propositions that comprise most of its organizational soul:

- The agency's main purpose, formulated by the 1981–1983 board and staff, has remained the steadfast principal guide and inspiration for Larkin Street's many strategic and operating decisions over the years: "To create a continuum of services that inspire youth to move beyond the streets. We will nurture potential, promote dignity, and support bold steps by all."

- Homeless youth need and deserve our help. They are on the streets through no fault of their own.

- Homeless youth will be vulnerable to adult abuses and society's demands if they are not provided with the means of achieving stability, self-confidence, socialization skills, education, employment skills, and life skills.

- Youth are resilient. Most homeless youth want to have a future beyond the streets, have dreams and ambitions for themselves, and will respond positively and responsibly to opportunities to restart their lives once they trust the adults and institutions around them, learn enough about possibilities for themselves, and are provided steady and reliable support.

- Never give up. Considerable struggle characterizes the process of emancipation from street life and of forging a positive and grounded transition to a more promising future. False starts, backward slippage, frustration, lost confidence, and depression accompany each youth's journey. Hope and determination are the antidotes.

- Youth need to access a continuum of support services to create sustained momentum for emancipation from street life toward productive and satisfying adulthood. Shelter, medical care, substance abuse counseling, education counseling, and job readiness preparation by themselves are insufficient.

- A passionate, full-fledged team effort must create and then backstop the continuum of support needed by the youth. The team encompasses dedicated professional staff that administer programs and provide caring warmth directly to the youth; a strong administrative infrastructure encompassing research and evaluation, development, and finance and control; a board of directors that supports the staff and agency through oversight, fundraising, and strategic perspective; volunteers who supplement and complement the staff's and board's capabilities; government agencies that provide programmatic funding and other resources; and concerned citizens, foundations, and businesses that invest their funds in the youth and the agency. Absent any one of these constituencies and contributions, Larkin Street could not operate effectively.

The story of Larkin Street is stirring and heroic. It exemplifies the extraordinary possibilities of offering hope, compassion, and a pathway to coping[1] for large numbers of otherwise hopeless individuals. It demonstrates that when concerned and generous citizens team with talented, professional staff, civic-minded businesses, charitable foundations, and public monies to address societal problems, notable progress can be made.

---

[1] During my recent visit to Larkin Street's special facility for homeless youth with HIV/AIDS, I noted the house rules on a blackboard in the main lounge: no personal attacks, general respect, no talking down to each other, one person at a time speaks, no yelling, what is said in group stays in group: confidentiality. Nearby on a bulletin board were announcements of meetings and organizations available to the youth: life after meth; men's support group; battering in relationships; job readiness class; free phone program to your family; LGBTQ organization; Haight Ashbury alcohol, sex, sobriety for men; job fair; deaf aids support group; quit smoking clinic; GED classes; Native American Health Center.

Sisters of Mercy

South Sudan is reputedly one of the harshest and poorest places in the world. Its temperature often exceeds 110 degrees Fahrenheit. About 90 percent of its population live on less than $1 day. There is little commerce to sustain its inhabitants. South Sudan has little running water, few paved roads, and minimal health care. And almost daily, conflicts arise between tribes and clans over cattle.

The 22 years of civil war that ravaged Sudan resulted in 2 million fatalities and 4.9 million internally displaced persons in the South—the highest number in the world. Most citizens fled their homes to avoid random killings, rape, pillage, torture, abduction of children, and forced military service for young males. It has been said that South Sudan is "a place fit only for missionaries, mercenaries, and misfits."

In this setting, women are culturally and economically oppressed. A girl growing up in South Sudan is more likely to die in childbirth than to receive five years of primary education. Only seven percent of women are literate or know their human rights. One in six pregnant women die before or during childbirth. A longstanding economic and cultural tradition is that girls' legal status is less than that of cows, as cattle are a family's most prized possession. Young girls are required to spend their days fetching water for their families from nearby streams and rivers and looking after their family's grazing cows or goats. Families view daughters as a source of income: When they reach 12 or 13, girls are bartered off for marriage to villagers for a dowry of cows. The girls are then destined for roles as caregivers to their new families and are expected to bear children, despite the inherent danger in doing so.

In 1997, some of South Sudan's young girls saw a ray of hope when the country's first all-girls school, St. Bakhita, a primary school for girls in kindergarten through eighth grade, was founded. Located in a remote village that is a three-hour drive from the border with Northern Kenya, St. Bakhita's students came from 24 tribes, most of whom had been displaced by the civil war. By 2009, the school had grown to include 800 girls, half of them boarders and the others local residents, who walked up to two hours through rugged countryside to and from school each day. In many instances, the families and caretakers of the students were initially attracted to St. Bakhita's by the free lunch that was served each day.[2] But, over time, girls who attended the school on a continuing basis grew to love learning and aspired to continue on to high school and enter careers in teaching or health care.

---

[2] A monthly highlight at the school was a small lunch serving of goat meat. The meat from ten goats fed the entire student body.

Then, in the spring of 2010, the World Food Program unexpectedly terminated its school feeding program in Sudan, apparently to divert its scarce resources to Sudanese villages suffering from famine. Without food for the girls, St. Bakhita's had to close, thus sending its students back to their families, who were intent on marrying them off for dowries. Upon hearing of St. Bakhita's plight, a small, recently founded San Francisco Bay Area not-for-profit organization, Mercy Beyond Borders (MBB), stepped up. MBB had "adopted" St. Bahkita's in 2008. When the organization heard of the crisis, it forwarded $10,000 in stopgap funding so the school could purchase food for the girls and reopen its doors.

Mercy Beyond Borders was founded by Sister Marilyn Lacey, who had spent 25 years working in refugee camps in Thailand and Kenya. She also helped refugees from all over the world resettle in the United States. Sister Marilyn, who was recognized by the Dalai Lama as an "Unsung Hero of Compassion" for her advocacy for refugees, is a member of the Sisters of Mercy. This organization was founded in Dublin, Ireland, in the nineteenth century by a wealthy heiress, Catherine McAuley, who was compassionately moved to help the poor, sick, and ignorant (particularly women and children) through the use of her station, financial resources, advocacy, and vision. Sisters of Mercy now ministers in 47 countries. Though decentralized organizationally into nine groups worldwide that rely on local autonomy to respond and adapt to the specific needs of an area or country, the Sisters are strongly united through their common inspiration and respect for their founder and her high-minded, compassionate, courageous, generous, and determined work with the poor and abandoned.

The Sisters of Mercy Constitution emphasizes the Sisters' obligation of "responding to a call to serve the needy." Following its founder's example, Sisters of Mercy reaches out to those in need with a spirit of hospitality to welcome all; innovation in how they seek to help the needy; a high level of professionalism and high standards in the services they render; and a collaborative spirit by which they seek to partner with others and to connect the affluent with poor and needy individuals. The organization's credo is "to serve wisely and compassionately in support of human dignity and the common good." Always focused on relieving misery and addressing causes of suffering, the Sisters of Mercy has sought to model mercy and justice and promote systemic change—all with a global perspective. The "charism" of Sisters of Mercy, as they refer to it, is a special spirit and vitality to help the poor that the Sisters believe is a gift from God.[3]

---

[3] Sisters of Mercy of the Americas Constitution

The organization's courage, boldness, and willingness to send nuns to distant outposts wherever the needy are and its commitment to minister mercy were heroically reflected when eight Sisters of Mercy arrived in San Francisco in 1854, four years after California had become a state and Northern California was a rough-and-tumble Gold Rush society. Soon after their arrival, an Asian cholera epidemic spread through San Francisco, and the eight nuns went into action: "In a crowded, panicky, demoralized hospital and city, the Sisters provided able and calming nursing services—even as the California legislature withdrew any responsibility for the indigent sick. When asked by the San Francisco Board of Supervisors, the Sisters of Mercy organized and operated the first county hospital." And again, in 1868, when San Francisco suffered a smallpox epidemic, the Sisters of Mercy cared for the ill. They also opened a new San Francisco hospital during the Civil War years, then a shelter for unemployed girls, a home for the homeless, a night school for adult classes, and an industrial school in which thousands of women learned skills, thereby helping immigrant families adjust to their new country.[4] Sister Mary Ann Scofield of the Sisters' Burlingame, California convent described the organization in this way: "We are active. We jump into problems. When we are face-to-face with the poor, we *immediately* want to help."

When Sister Marilyn Lacey founded Mercy Beyond Borders, her vision was well aligned with the 180-year history, principles, and spirit of the Sisters of Mercy. Mercy Beyond Borders' humanitarian and compassionate purpose was to bring immediate relief, hope, income possibilities, and education to displaced women and girls. Longer-term, the organization's aim was to bring about gender equity, justice, and the strengthening of societal foundations through the positive influences that educated women could bring to family and village life and structure.[5] Helping St. Bahkita School reopen in impoverished South Sudan was another instance, in a very long list worldwide, where the influence and dedication of Sisters of Mercy intervened to stand with and improve the lot of the poor.

Both Larkin Street Youth Services and Sisters of Mercy are devoted to saving lives. Both have touched the hearts of the caring people who have joined their ranks, delivered great service and relief to those they serve, and have enabled both caregivers and recipients to discover great meaning, passion, and satisfaction in their lives. In the twenty-first century, millions of individuals, thousands of organizations, and entire societies search for greater meaning, rewarding outlets for their capabilities and passions, and greater satisfaction

---

[4] Rose McArdle S.M., *Mercy Undaunted: 125 Years in California* (Burlingame, CA: Sisters of Mercy, 1979).

[5] By 2010, MBB's mission was "Partnering with displaced women and girls in ways that alleviate their extreme poverty."

for their lives. What is it about Larkin Street and Sisters of Mercy—and by extension, thousands of virtuous not-for-profit and non-governmental organizations in our society[6]—that unleashes such passion and commitment to these causes and engenders such meaning, fulfillment, and vitality in the human spirit?

Both of these not-for-profit organizations can be seen to have at their core a driving force that is a source of their vitality, a special character, and a transcendent idea.

Noted earlier, Larkin Street's is comprised of a mixture of core principles:

- A concern for homeless youth
- A dedication that focuses available efforts and resources on helping the youth gain hope and move beyond the streets
- Belief in the youths' vulnerability and resilience
- Understanding of the programmatic elements needed to save homeless youth

Meanwhile, Sisters of Mercy operates on its own core principles:

- A call from God
- The inspiration and example of its founder
- Total lifelong commitment
- Devotion to works of mercy
- Living closely with the poor—particularly women and children—and being devoted to their needs
- Participation in the life of their religious community
- A willingness to travel to outposts (no matter how harsh) to help the poor and sick

University of Notre Dame

The University of Notre Dame is a 170-year-old institution whose founder, Rev. Edward Sorin, C.S.C., emigrated from France to North America in the early 1840s with the Congregation of the Holy Cross, a young French

---

[6] In California, an estimated 935 million hours of volunteer time was contributed in 2010. Source: "The Health Benefits of Volunteering: A Review of Research," Corporation for National and Community Service 2010; cited in Blue Shield of California, *Better Living Newsletter* (Spring/Summer 2011), p. 7.

missionary order. Father Sorin wrote at the university's founding (on an Indiana site where a log cabin marked an old mission outpost): "This college will be one of the most powerful means for doing good in this country." True to Father Sorin's word, the university's current mission statement reflects its ongoing dedication to good works:

> The University seeks to cultivate in its students not only an appreciation for the great achievements of human beings, but also a disciplined sensibility to the poverty, injustice, and oppression that burden the lives of so many.[7] The aim is to create a sense of human solidarity and concern for the common good that will bear fruit as learning becomes service to justice.

Notre Dame's concerted commitment to performing good works has been a cornerstone for the university since its founding in 1842, when Sorin's young congregation began providing care for the local Potawatomi tribes. The university's spirit of service and volunteerism has only grown stronger with the passage of time. In many ways, members of the Notre Dame community (warmly referred to as the "Notre Dame family" by those affiliated with the university) feel a personal responsibility to help the university fulfill its mission of providing service to others. In fact, volunteerism is so woven into the fabric of university life at Notre Dame that nearly 80 percent of its undergraduates find a way to give back to the community, whether by volunteering at local organizations that serve the poor, traveling abroad to provide disaster-relief assistance to those in developing countries, or dedicating themselves in their post-collegiate endeavors to service-oriented organizations such as Teach for America and the Peace Corps. In 1983, in order to facilitate the Notre Dame community's efforts to do good, the university established the Center for Social Concerns (CSC) on campus to provide students and faculty access to community-based learning courses, community-based research, and service opportunities. Preceded by the Notre Dame Office of Volunteer Services and the Center for Experiential Learning, the CSC is one of the most frequented buildings on campus; and undergraduates, graduate students, and faculty can often be found meeting with representatives from some of the 50 local service organizations with whom the CSC maintains a relationship.

Members of the Notre Dame community also feel inspired to engage in volunteerism by the many Notre Dame leaders and visionaries who have dedicated their lives to the service of others. One leader in particular stands out as a living testament to Sorin's commitment—Rev. Theodore Hesburgh,

---

[7] In 2011, Notre Dame remained the only major U.S. university that forbade license holders (such as Adidas) to put the school's logo on any product made in China because China does not permit independent labor unions. Source: "Notre Dame Alone Among Schools on China Goods Ban," *San Francisco Chronicle*, May 18, 2011.

C.S.C., who served as Notre Dame's president for 35 years. Despite the fact that he is undoubtedly one of the most influential Catholic priests of the twentieth century, Hesburgh is always gracious and eager to converse with members of the Notre Dame family. (When asked about the various highlights from the time they spent on campus, many university alumni will fondly recall the chance encounters they had had with Father Ted, as he is affectionately known on campus.) His humanitarian work and commitment to seeking out social justice are well-known, and members of the university community take pride in the fact that one of their own dedicated his life to raising up those who are downtrodden by society. Among his many good deeds, Hesburgh served as a member and later was chairman of the U.S. Civil Rights Commission; advocated for the elimination of nuclear arms and organized meetings that brought together scientists and theologians who opposed the use of atomic weapons; developed a federal government–private industry effort that averted mass starvation in Cambodia; and served on the Anti-Incitement Committee established by the Wye Plantation Treaty to mute Israeli-Palestinian tension. Without a doubt, Hesburgh's active dedication to solving the world's many problems moves those in the Notre Dame community who feel similarly called to seek out social justice.

Unlike some other colleges where community service is a mandatory condition for graduation, Notre Dame students are by no means required to provide service to others. Yet, they continue to give their time, energy, and talents because, as their peers, professors, and the university leadership have taught them, it's considered the right thing to do. Service work gives the Notre Dame community a shared sense of identity, makes its members feel they are part of something larger than themselves, gives them the opportunity to live up to high ideals, and cements the bond that Notre Dame alumni, faculty, staff, and students share.

The university's soul, as explained by its current president, Rev. John I. Jenkins, C.S.C., encompasses the founder's dedication to a higher purpose: to serve as a beacon of hope and a symbol of the "American Dream" to generations of immigrants while retaining Catholicism's emphasis on community and distinction.[8] How does that the university achieve its purpose? By adhering to the following commitments:

- Serving as a Catholic place[9] of teaching, research, scholarship, and publication

---

[8] At the university's 1842 founding, Father Sorin vowed that he would build the greatest Catholic university in the world.

[9] 85 percent of the undergraduates are Catholic.

- Instilling a rich sense of community[10] that enables students, faculty, alumni, and staff to share their lives

- Retaining a committed sense of meaningful higher purpose obtained largely through service[11]

- Holding true to a long tradition of engagement with the wider society about the issues of the day (for example, civil rights)[12]

- Committing to the pursuit of academic and athletic excellence and distinction on a national stage

Over the years, Notre Dame has grown in stature and renown to become a leading undergraduate teaching institution ranked among the top 25 U.S. institutions of higher learning, where 80 percent of its students are active in social services and at least 10 percent of each year's baccalaureate graduating class devote at least one year to volunteer services.[13] Its athletic teams consistently rank among the nation's finest, and its alumni are exceedingly strong supporters of the university.

Stanford University

Leland Stanford Junior University was founded in 1881 by Senator Leland and Jane Stanford in memory of their only child, who died as a teenager. The Stanfords gave their 8,800-acre Palo Alto Farm and more than $10 million ("the largest endowment in the history of mankind" at that time)[14] to fund a great university "for the children of California who would become their children" so that California could thrive by having very well-educated, useful, and idealistic citizens. The Stanfords promised that the future of California's children would "be better; they are needed to make it better, and a legacy of

---

[10] 80 percent of the students live on campus, one of the highest undergraduate residential concentrations of any national university.

[11] Notre Dame's Alliance for Catholic Education sends approximately 200 recent graduates to teach in understaffed Catholic schools in various states; through the University's Social Concerns Seminars, undergraduates devote their semester breaks to providing assistance in Appalachia and other impoverished areas.

[12] It has always stood for values in a world of facts. One of Notre Dame's goals is to provide a forum where the various lines of Catholic thought can intersect with all forms of knowledge in open discussion. Note: These facts about Notre Dame and those contained in the three preceding footnotes are from the university's website and publications from the Office of Undergraduate Admissions.

[13] Since the Peace Corps' 1961 founding, more than 800 Notre Dame graduates have been volunteers—more than from any other Catholic college or university.

[14] As proclaimed at the time by London's *Daily Telegraph*.

education will serve them more than any other."[15] Stanford University began as a tuition-free, non-sectarian institution of higher learning that was open to women and men of all means. In each of these respects, Stanford University was importantly different from many universities in the East.

From the early days of Stanford University's founding through today, contributing to the world's bank of knowledge in important ways, helping to solve the great problems and issues of the day, and striving for excellence in all that it does[16] have been driving forces and expectations at Stanford.

Because Leland Stanford was a very successful businessman and builder, because both he and Jane Stanford were products of the pioneering West, and because California was a land of opportunity and creation, an important aspect of Stanford University's soul has been its entrepreneurial, innovative, and pioneering spirit. Founded more than 100 years later than many fine Eastern educational establishments, Stanford was unfettered by many East Coast societal traditions and was continually invigorated and supported not just by the "winning of the West" context in which it is set but also by California's spirit of openness. Stanford's approaches to education and to its relationships with alumni, communities, and businesses relied on being experimental and possessing a frontier and pioneering freshness (the university's informal motto, "The wind of freedom blows," began with its first president) that is characterized by a "we can do anything" spirit. As prompted by Senator Stanford, "If I thought the University was to be only like the others in this country, I had better have given the money to some existing institution. I want it to be on a different plane."[17] And in a 1904 letter from Jane Stanford to the university's trustees: "Let us not be afraid to outgrow old thoughts and ways and dare to think on new lines as to the work under our care. Let us not be poor copies of other universities. Let us be progressive."[18]

Stanford's soul is explained partially in terms of its service to others (in co-founder Jane Stanford's words, "A desire to render the greatest possible service to mankind") and by its founders' values and vision. As a secular

---

[15] Source: The Founding Grant Society of Stanford University.

[16] In the university's founding grant in 1885, Leland and Jane Stanford charged the board of trustees and all of their successors to maintain the highest standards of teaching and research. Cited by Isaac Stein, chair, board of trustees, in Stanford's *2002 Annual Report*, p. 16. And, that the university should "promote the public welfare by exercising an influence on behalf of humanity and civilization." Cited by President John Hennessy in the *Stanford Alumni Magazine* (January/February 2004), p. 6.

[17] As quoted in Susan Weis, *Stanford: A Portrait of a University* (Stanford Alumni Association: 1999).

[18] Quoted by John Hennessy, President of Stanford University in the *Stanford Alumni Magazine*.

institution founded with the highest academic goals, extensive resources, and a location situated in the wide open and emerging West, much of Stanford's key sources of vitality and meaning reflect the founders' aspirations and the circumstances under which the university has matured.

The university's soul also includes the origins and nature of its location. "The Farm" (as it has always been called) has a strong family feeling that binds generations of students, graduates, faculty, and administrators together. And with its vast 8,000-plus acres[19] of rolling hills and palm and eucalyptus trees, all of which are located in the foothills of California, its setting creates a sense of quietude and well-being.

Today, Stanford is widely considered to be one of the world's finest universities in terms of its student body, faculty, and facilities. Its endowment ranks third among all U.S. universities. All around, its athletic program is the nation's best. The Farm continues to be one of America's most magnificent campuses and boasts state-of-the-art facilities. The university's alumni are notably loyal and devoted supporters.[20] Relationships between Stanford and nearby Silicon Valley firms have continued since the 1940s to be close and mutually beneficial.[21] Stanford alums and faculty have been significant leaders and contributors to the world's economic, social, cultural, and scientific advancements. The university is very grounded in its sense of excellence. And these are just a handful of Stanford's notable accomplishments.

San Francisco International Airport

The final not-for-profit organization in this chapter is a public sector enterprise—San Francisco International Airport, SFO, as it is popularly called, is the world's nineteenth largest airport and the ninth largest in the United States. In 2011, SFO accommodated 41 million passengers (approximately 112,000 per day) and more than 1,100 daily aircraft landings and takeoffs. With an annual budget of more than $700 million that is self-funded[22] through its current operations, and a dedicated white- and blue-collar staff of approximately 1,550 employees, SFO is generally regarded by the aviation

---

[19] The university's founding grant required that none of the "Farm's" land ever be sold.

[20] In 2009, Stanford raised more money in a single year than any other college or university: $640 million.

[21] Indeed, Stanford Engineering Professor Frederick Terman is widely credited for having mentored his students Hewlett and Packard and suggested their first marketable product as part of his vision of a knowledge-based region centered around Stanford. David Jacobson, "Founding Fathers," *Stanford Alumni Magazine* (July/August 1998): pp. 58–61.

[22] SFO does not require taxpayers' funds and annually makes a dividend payment to the city's general fund calculated at 15 percent of concession revenue ($30.2 million in 2011).

industry, travel publications, business travelers, and airlines as one of North America's top three airports and among the world's ten best.[23] Its $5 billion Airport Commission revenue bonds are rated A+ by Fitch.

To serve its two principal customers—passengers and airlines—and to comply fully with extensive governmental regulations[24] and aviation industry conventions, SFO must self-manage to exceedingly high levels of quality and consistency 24 hours a day, 365 days a year. The airport also requires adaptability when confronted with extraordinary external circumstances such as 9/11, significant fluctuations in the number of airline passengers, major airline bankruptcies, terrorist threats, and disruptions of other natures.

SFO's ability to perform consistently at a very high level reflects well-designed management and administrative practices and notable continuity in most airport leadership positions (there have been only two SFO airport directors in 30 years). The airport's operational excellence is further bolstered by the exceptional commitment demonstrated by much of the airport's white-collar and blue-collar workforce, and SFO's ability to work successfully within San Francisco's elaborate Civil Service regulations and processes, as well as with 29 labor unions.[25]

As John L. Martin, SFO's airport director, explained: "Commission employees at all levels are physically present every day, interacting with the airport. It gives all of us continual awareness of the airport in action, a sense of pride in our operations and in our beautiful and majestic facilities; and is a continuing reminder of the importance of serving customers and making our city proud. We are the initial and last impressions of San Francisco for passengers, and we want to do our part for our proud city."

Although SFO is not an organizational culture with a high degree of socializing among its employees, SFO employees love working at the airport. They like being part of an organization that is at the forefront of its industry, and they feel strongly committed to SFO's highest-level goals.[26] Indeed, SFO's mission ("We provide an exceptional airport in service to our communities"),

---

[23] As examples: "Best Airport in North America 2008" by Skytrax, the aviation industry's leading independent quality research organization; recipient of IATA's prestigious Eagle Award (only the third time in history to have been awarded to a U.S. airport); "Best U.S. Airport for Business Travelers" by Arthur Frommer and MSNBC; the newly renovated Terminal 2 was the first LEED Gold-registered renovated airport terminal in the United States; "Airport with Best Overall Concession Program" by 2012 Airport Revenue News Best Concession Awards.

[24] Thirty different federal, state, regional, and local agencies have jurisdictions over some aspects of airport operations or property.

[25] All SFO Airport Commission employees belong to a union.

[26] It would be possible to manage an urban airport to only "acceptable" standards in service and facilities as long as its cost to airlines was competitive.

aspirational vision ("Reaching for Number 1"), and its core values all reflect great pride, commitment, dedication, and high ideals:

We are one team.

We treat everyone with respect.

We communicate fully and help one another.

We strive to be the best.

We are open to new ideas.[27]

We are innovative.

We are committed to SFO being a great place to work.

We are each responsible for the airport's success.

We take pride in SFO and in our accomplishments.

SFO's soul comprises the commitment by everyone involved to operate an outstanding airport; the pride in SFO that accompanies that commitment; the distinctive San Francisco identity in SFO's décor, restaurants, gift stores, and museum; and ingrained beliefs held by commission employees that it operates one of the best airports, is one of the best San Francisco government departments; and provides outstanding service to customers. SFO's soul also comprises the beauty, distinctiveness, and majesty of key airport buildings, their interiors (particularly the International Terminal and T-2),[28] and SFO's airport museum; and the imprint of its long-serving airport director, John Martin, one of the industry's most respected leaders who has served 15 years as director and 30 years as SFO Commission employee under six different San Francisco mayors. Stories abound about how Martin knows everything that is going on at SFO, thanks to his daily walks around the airport and his calls to responsible parties to immediately fix whatever is wrong—ranging from a burned-out light bulb in the parking garage, to slow moving security lines, to discourteous curbside attendants, to overly priced products in food stalls. SFO employees admire his desire to continually push for improvements in SFO's customer services, to lead the industry with cutting-edge ideas, to always do what's best for SFO, and to be fair.

---

[27] Opened in 2000 at a cost of $1 billion, the International Terminal was purpose-built to accommodate the huge airplane of the future (for example, Airbus 380), even though none of these large aircraft began flying until late 2007. "SFO's Gigantic Payoff," *San Francisco Chronicle*, May 14, 2011, pp. D1, D6.

[28] Terminal 2 (T-2) reopened in April 2011 and "was designed to make it a model of sustainable development and relaxing travel. We want to return the romance to travel, make it less stressful." "Terminal 2 Takes Off," *San Francisco Chronicle*, April 7, 2011, pp. A1, A12.

Examples of Ingredients in Business Organizations' Souls

Business organizations, indeed, can have souls as exemplified by the six leading U.S. firms that are described in this chapter: Barclays Global Investors, Merrill Lynch, Levi Strauss & Company, Wells Fargo, Dodge & Cox, and Williams-Sonoma, Inc.

Barclays Global Investors

At the time of its 2009 acquisition by BlackRock, Inc., Barclays Global Investors (BGI) managed more than $1 trillion in client assets. In addition, the firm was the world's largest institutional fund manager, the leading index investment manager,[1] and the world's largest participant in exchange-traded funds for the

---

[1] BGI (including its antecedents) was one of the two firms that taught the professional institutional and retail worlds about the potential benefits of passive index fund investing. The other firm was Vanguard.

retail investor marketplace, with about $400 billion in such assets. What contributed to BGI's many years of rapid growth and to the firm's massive levels of success? Importantly, how did the firm's founding story and original *raison d'être* to offer its clients a revolutionary set of investment products and services become the core of its soul? Pattie Dunn, who joined Wells Fargo Investment Advisors (which later became BGI) a few years after the firm's founding and became co-chairman of the firm in 1995 and CEO in 1998, provided some answers to these vital questions in interviews with the author.

"In BGI's earliest years as Wells Fargo Investment Advisors," Dunn explained, "a core group of leaders tussled with what kind of firm BGI should be. The group, which included Jim Vertin, who headed the business; John 'Mac' McQuown, the head of the bank's Management Sciences Unit; Bill Fouse, the head of Wells Fargo Investment Advisors' Investment Systems Group; Bill Jahnke of the Financial Analysis Department; and, at times, consultants Barr Rosenburg and subsequent Nobel Prize Winner in Economics William Sharpe, debated at length about how to rigorously apply advances in investment theory and high-speed computer processing to produce a better investment outcome for clients." Dunn continued, "Vertin was a traditional investment manager who became disillusioned with conventional investment management practices and was willing to sponsor the development of what he referred to as 'the new knowledge' coming out of academia. McQuown was a tech-savvy financial products intellectual. Fouse was a creative investment professional with a sense for how to transform esoteric investment theory into practical investment solutions. And Jahnke," Dunn concluded, "developed concepts and capabilities for managing computerized investment portfolios.

"The underlying question was, 'What kind of firm was it going to be: a traditional fund manager that relied on stock picking? Or one that relied on new, unproven applications of hard-to-grasp academic theory (based on the recently evolved Efficient Market Hypothesis for explaining market behavior and price changes) for which there was no apparent marketplace demand but which had the potential to create a more reliable and less expensive way to manage money—an opportunity to change the world of money management to 'passive' index investing.

"After the lengthy and energetic series of debates," Dunn explained, "there evolved a spirit of pioneering, a mission of providing a better way to manage money, and a sense that if we didn't 'carry the torch,' there was no one else as committed and capable to do so." As Dunn and Jahnke further emphasized, "This matters! If we succeed, the world will be a better place!" (Many years hence, BGI's vision statement reflected this grand and bold notion: "We seek to create financial freedom for millions of individuals and thousands of organizations around the world.")

Dunn continued, "From then on, we sought to be the most advanced and capable investment manager on the planet. Our employees had a sense of intellectual arrogance and took great delight as we pitched our theoretical approach against what we saw as the practical shortcomings of competitors' investment management products and services.[2] There was *zeal* among the bright, energetic, and nice young employees that populated the growing firm. They had 'fire in the belly,' a phrase that was popularized in the firm by its able, brainy, longtime CEO, Fred Grauer. Employees really believed in what they were doing and worked hard and intelligently for the firm's success. Our firm's values were knowledge, trust, passion, and creativity. Over all of the years," Dunn concluded, "beginning with having to convince the marketplace as we competed with the traditional fund managers, and more recently while competing with quantitative fund managers, I seriously doubt the firm would have had lasting commercial success without this core 'soul' it carried with it."

Over time, BGI's strong belief in and pursuit of a better way to manage money led to big changes in the investment management industry. Despite the fact that "passive" indices were virtually nonexistent when BGI's antecedent, Wells Fargo Investment Advisors, began business in 1973, more than $4 trillion was invested worldwide in these investment vehicles by 2012. Of that total, about $1.2 trillion was accounted for by more than 1,400 U.S. exchange-traded funds. In a broader context, 44 cents out of every dollar invested worldwide in conventionally managed funds was placed in index and exchange-traded funds. On the cost side, according to Morningstar, Inc., the average asset-weighted expense ratio for U.S. stock index funds and ETFs was 0.19 percent versus 0.92 percent for actively managed funds.[3] When BGI began energetically commercializing its ETFs ("iShares") in 2000 and bringing them to the attention of the broader investing public, only a few other firms, including State Street Global Advisors, offered such a product. These extraordinary changes in investor appetite, fund management approaches, and passive investment expenses were in no small part due to the influential pioneering role that BGI and its antecedent, Wells Fargo Investment Advisors, played in the investment arena. Elements of BGI's soul thus had not only benefitted the firm, but they had also helped to transform the investment management industry and investors' well-being.

---

[2] In 1973, the firm opened its first index-comingled fund with $5 million from Wells Fargo's Pension Fund and $5 million from Illinois Bell. Ten years later, its indexing business had grown to nearly $12 billion in assets as the concept caught on with pension funds. After another ten years, the firm had amassed $155 billion. "BGI Thinks Big," *Institutional Investor* (April 1997), pp. 62–72.

[3] *Wall Street Journal*, April 23–24, 2011, p. B9.

Dodge & Cox

Similar to BGI, Dodge & Cox is a highly successful firm that is dedicated to providing its clients with high-quality "active" investment management services. One of the largest privately owned investment managers in the world, Dodge & Cox's longstanding source of vital energy and much of its soul consist of enduring principles and core beliefs that relate to the approach it takes to doing its work as one of the industry's first traditional investment managers. The list below offers a look at the foundational tenets and many elements of its soul that drive Dodge & Cox's business activities:

- Put clients' interests first[4]

- Remain independently owned (As explained by a senior portfolio manager, "When we think about to whom we report, who is our boss; it is our *clients*, not another organization. We ask each new employee to think of themselves as an *owner*: How can you make this organization better for serving our clients?")

- Maintain a long-term perspective ("We manage portfolios in the same way as we manage employees—with a long-term perspective. We intentionally try to recruit people that fit with our culture and will be interested in staying here for the rest of their careers," explained a long-time employee.)

- Utilize extensive bottom-up research on individual companies as the basis for investment decisions

- Vet investment proposals with a large number of the firm's investment professionals in order to generate the best possible ideas and ensure cautious investment decision-making. This team approach is incorporated into everything the firm does. (In the words of a Dodge & Cox analyst, "Our culture is very collegial and collaborative, built on trust, respect, and a belief that more brains are better than one. We need people who have the strength to advocate ideas and are willing to give and take with our team process, and use a long-run perspective.")

---

[4] For example, Harry Hagey, the firm's CEO in the late twentieth century, continued to be the principal account manager for a private client he had served for 30 years—even though the account had only $200,000 in assets and Hagey oversaw billions of dollars invested through the firm.

- Make changes in how the firm operates only infrequently and cautiously[5]

Dodge & Cox is widely respected for a litany of reasons. It refuses to compromise its integrity.[6] It is committed to aligning its own interests with its clients' interests at all times. It consistently achieves superior investment results. It boasts a long-tenured staff[7] but retains the ability to attract top university graduates. It has established overall stability and financial success through many investment cycles. It has enjoyed long-term growth since its 1933 founding. For these reasons and more, Dodge & Cox is one of the traditional investment management industry's blue-chip firms.

Merrill Lynch

Merrill Lynch, which began in 1915, has grown to become America's largest brokerage businesses and is credited with "bringing Wall Street to Main Street" after World War II. The soul of the firm grew out of founder Charlie Merrill's 1941 "ten commandments," which were formalized and promulgated in 1992 by then-CEO Dan Tully as the "Merrill Lynch Principles" and included client focus, respect for the individual, teamwork, responsible citizenship, and integrity. Along with the ten commandments, the brokerage's origins also played an important role in fostering the soul of Merrill Lynch.

Merrill Lynch was built by an immigrant population of managers and brokers, and their immigrant roots were a strong source of Merrill's self-identity and culture. As a career Merrill Lynch employee who rose through the retail brokerage ranks in New York City and ultimately became a corporate senior vice president related: "We were a feisty group—mostly Irish Catholics and Jews. We could disagree without being disagreeable with each other. After work, we would lock arms and belly up to the bar together. We were the 'maverick' firm. The other Wall Street firms had privileged guys as leaders—Ivy Leaguers. Most of our employees had to earn their way in the world. We

---

[5] There was long-standing organizational pride in not changing and in promulgating institutional stability.

[6] "We want to do what is in the best long-term interests of our clients, regardless of whether or not we are legally obliged to do so or not. I would call it 'doing what's right even when no one's looking'; we readily admit mistakes. No one is punished for speaking the truth," explained a senior portfolio manager.

[7] One of the reasons Dodge & Cox employees consider the firm to be an attractive employer is its policy of encouraging healthy life balance. "We want a *career* contribution from people, so it's not in anyone's best interest to burn people out. Having many other-than-work dimensions to our lives and good work/life balance helps everyone pick up their game," said a 23-year Dodge & Cox veteran.

were self-made and appreciated the work opportunity. All of us were ambitious and willing to cold call prospects. When we got through, we felt proud."

The can-do and underdog spirit that this employee describes experiencing at Merrill Lynch became the foundation upon which the brokerage firm developed its culture. Even Merrill Lynch's CEOs fit this hardworking, self-made mold. "Merrill's CEOs all came from modest families. They were 'real' people," said a ten-year Merrill Lynch London executive, who had transferred in from Citibank. "They worked hard and worked their way up in Merrill Lynch. There was some sense of being the underdog versus Morgan Stanley or Goldman Sachs. It didn't matter what school one went to. We had pride that we weren't 'white-shoe.'" "We loved being the underdog," said another Merrill Lynch veteran, "and doing things others thought we couldn't accomplish."

Merrill Lynch's scrappy, we'll-show-them! sense of enthusiasm isn't the only defining attribute of its organizational core. The hardworking underdog identity created a powerful sense of camaraderie and esprit de corps that extended all the way from the bottom-most, entry-level employees up to the CEOs. "All around us was a sense that we were all in it together … a common person's firm … there was no arrogance. We could count on each other. We were good people who looked out for each other. It was us versus 'the Street.' We could accomplish what we wanted," related a longtime Merrill Lynch employee in greater New York City who rose to become a corporate officer. Said another employee, "We wanted to come to work. Our colleagues were friends, and we knew their families. We had a strong sense of family and belonging."

Employees felt that Merrill Lynch was the rare meritocracy on Wall Street. As one executive put it, "It's about one's performance. Results speak loudest. It's *not* about being Ivy League or having wealthy backgrounds." There was a mutual understanding between the company and employees that, while the performance expectations were high, "Mother Merrill" would take care of those who performed. "We were expected to work hard. If we did, we would succeed," said one employee. He continued, "'Mother Merrill' was a general sense that the company would always be there for you as an individual. 'I'm going to take care of you; you take care of what you're supposed to.'" As another former executive put it, "'Mother Merrill' was the feeling that we worked for a *family*. We cared for other employees and clients. We felt a kinship. We liked each other. We loved to socialize with each other. We loved attending off-sites. If we were a fraternity, 'Mother Merrill' would have been the fraternity's name."

Merrill Lynch stood clearly for a set of values that employees embraced, and this bond created an immense sense of loyalty and pride. "We were about character, spirit, leadership, ethics, and pride. We were not about bricks and mortar and cold numbers. We were proud of our principles inherited from Charlie Merrill. The interest of the customer always came first. We were a team, and no one's ego was more important than the team. (As Bill Schreyer, a highly respected Merrill Lynch CEO, was apt to proclaim, 'Take your work seriously, but don't take yourself seriously.') We had respect for everyone. We had an obligation to support our broader community of which we were a part. Integrity was everything!" "These principles of Charlie Merrill were passed to my father," related Winthrop H. Smith, Jr., to a gathering of firm executives. Smith himself was a 28-year Merrill Lynch employee, son of one of the founding fathers, and a former senior executive of the firm.

"Most of us were 'lifers,' more than in any other Wall Street firm. We had enormous loyalty to Merrill Lynch," said a longtime employee. "'Mother Merrill' was a shorthand way of referring to the foundation of what we felt good about. It came from the top. We had a sense of belonging and feeling good. We weren't the best white-shoe firm, but we represented the people—we were not highbrow. We were proud of the "Thundering Herd" and the Bull. (Author's Note: For about 50 years, Merrill Lynch has used a bull as its logo and proclaimed itself "bullish on America" in advertising. Its large brokerage organization became widely known as The Thundering Herd.) We were proud to be a member." "We were raised in this business and grew up with the company," related a Midwestern office manager in the private client business in his thirty-eighth year with Merrill Lynch. "Everyone was proud to be a part. We aspired to Charlie Merrill's principles, and we always remember them. It's in our blood!"

"In 2008–2009, when the financial system and Merrill Lynch were said to be on the brink of extinction and various competing firms called to talk about my joining them," said a West Coast private client managing director, "I couldn't find anywhere else to go, because no firm had the soul Merrill Lynch does!"

Wells Fargo Bank

In 1998, when Norwest Bank (a large and mostly Midwestern super regional banking institution) acquired Wells Fargo Bank (a large, mostly Western states, banking institution), the combined entity represented more than 2,000 (!) smaller banks that had been acquired over more than 100 years by Norwest and Wells Fargo. At the time, the newly combined entity had approximately 5,000 offices, 120,000 employees, 19 million customers, $4 billion in net income, and $300 billion in assets. For Richard Kovacevich, who was CEO at the time of the 1998 merger, the key questions regarding the future of the firm were as follows: What kind of institution do its leaders want it to be? What character, values, principles, priorities, and culture will best bring together these two proud and successful financial institutions to create a highly successful, trusted, and respected national financial services firm?

Norwest Corporation, which until the merger had been headquartered in Minneapolis, was founded in 1929 and grew principally in the Midwest into a diversified financial services company through the acquisition of a large number of small- and medium-sized banks and financial services firms. From the mid-1980s on, Norwest's strategic focus on quality relationship banking and cross-selling was delivered through branches of well-trained and committed staff. Most of the growth Norwest experienced as a result of this strategy had been architected by Kovacevich, who had been recruited from an executive role in Citibank's Consumer Bank.

In contrast, Wells Fargo Bank, the oldest bank in the West, began in 1852 as a stagecoach and banking firm during the California Gold Rush. For about 65 years, the bank's principal commercial focus and its history, culture, and expansion were tied to a variety of express and related service businesses: buying and selling gold, safe keeping valuables, delivering mail and goods, transferring funds, and accepting deposits. The Pony Express, overland stage coaches, gold and silver mining, gun fights, the California Gold Rush, the birth of San Francisco, and the construction of the transcontinental railroad were all part of Wells Fargo's history, as was its serving as the principal communications conduit both among communities in the American West and between the West and the East. Then, at the start of World War I, the U.S. government nationalized the bank's express business and Wells Fargo refocused itself on the financial services business. For much of the twentieth century, Wells Fargo grew principally as a California retail commercial bank, opening branches as California grew, acquiring smaller banks, and developing specialties in agriculture and real estate. By the 1970s, with its familiar stagecoach logo, good customer service delivered by friendly branch bankers, and the overall positive growth of the California economy, Wells Fargo grew into a popular, well-regarded regional bank.

In 1998, after Kovacevich had assessed the histories, resources, capabilities, cultures, and marketplace positioning of the about-to-be-merged Norwest and Wells Fargo banks, he determined to "take the best from both banks." Many years earlier, when Kovacevich had become Norwest's leader in the mid-1980s, he concluded that several principles should be in place in order to have a successful financial institution:

1. Among a financial services institution's principal stakeholders, its employees deserve to be nourished by a strong and positive culture of respect, acknowledgement, teamwork, collegiality, and support;

2. Decisions to be made about the organization's culture and management practices needed to reflect the aspirations, ideas, and needs of its employees;

3. The bank's vision and values had to be thoughtfully and compellingly tied to its business model;

4. Employees needed helpful reminders and reinforcement about the institution's vision and values to keep them alive and strong.

Drawing upon these convictions, Kovacevich and his executive team had extensive discussions about what Norwest's aspirations and culture should look like. (One of its goals included becoming one of America's great companies when the bank was only of modest size.) He ultimately drafted the conclusions of these deliberations into a "Vision and Values" booklet intended for all Norwest employees. Over the years, the booklet was renewed and recirculated every two years, with very little change over time. The process was exceptionally well conceived, well regarded, and successful at Norwest.

Consequently, in the 1998 merger with Wells Fargo Bank, Kovacevich invoked the same approach again. He formed teams of managers and executives from both banks to work together to examine each business and support area. The team members of each organization also explained to their counterparts their legacy bank's history, culture, and values, and together they identified commonalities and differences and sought to determine what the new organization should be founded on. Kovacevich served as a facilitator, scribe, and ultimate decision maker—but not the creator—of the contents for the development of the new bank's "Vision and Values" booklet. The most important principles, beliefs, aspirations, and strategies of the institution and the connectivity between them were explained and communicated to all of the merged company's employees.

Decisions were made in 1998 to name the combined bank Wells Fargo, utilize San Francisco as the corporate headquarters, and use the Wells Fargo stagecoach as the corporate icon. (Over the long history of the legacy Wells Fargo Bank, the image of a six-horse stagecoach thundering across the American West evoked warm associations among Americans with the Old West and connoted reliability in the face of challenge, security, superior service, dependability, longevity, forward movement, power, and teamwork.) There was also a reaffirmation of the Norwest core belief that "employees are our most important asset and our competitive advantage."

When the new identity of the combined Norwest/Wells Fargo was rolled out among legacy Norwest customers and staff, great effort was made to highlight the historic importance of Wells Fargo in the Midwest's late 1880s development. Attention was paid to former Wells Fargo offices in various

Norwest cities; tales were recounted about local Wells Fargo agents; associations were celebrated between the ancestors of current-day Norwest customers and employees who had been Wells Fargo agents; and the fact was highlighted that William Fargo was one of Norwest's original investors.

Levi Strauss & Company

In the same era as the Gold Rush (1849), Wells Fargo's founding as an express business (1852), and the arrival of eight brave Sisters of Mercy in San Francisco (1854), Levi Strauss landed in the city in 1853 to open the West Coast office of the Strauss Brothers' dry goods wholesaling business, which had been founded six years earlier in New York by the new immigrant family. Twenty years later, Strauss and a Reno tailor, Jacob Davis, patented a new kind of exceedingly durable work pants for men—overalls—that became known 87 years later as "jeans." Together with his four Stern family nephews who joined him in business—and later inherited the company—Levi Strauss expanded the company's clothing product line for many years into a thriving business. Then, at the conclusion of World War I, Walter Haas, a Stern son-in-law, joined the business, as did his cousin, Daniel Koshland. The two worked closely and ultimately headed the company for 30 years.

Between 1985 and 1987, Robert Haas, the then-recently appointed Levi Strauss & Co. CEO and the great-great-grandnephew of Levi Strauss, convened a series of three separate training sessions for employees. These sessions were used to help a broad range of people understand the company's values and how they should be applied and guide workplace behavior. These training sessions also functioned as "learning laboratories," where management could learn more about employee concerns and understand where issues existed. Each off-site was comprised of white male managers, women, and minority employees, and the agenda included Diversity in the Workforce, Equal Opportunity Employment Goals and Realities, and Discrimination Experienced by Women and Minorities. The discussions were complex, difficult, and awkward. Ultimately, however, the discussions that took place during the diversity training sessions led to company-wide diversity aspirations, new employment practices, training for all managers, and greater accommodations to the needs of women and minority employees.

The corporate sensitivities and sensibilities demonstrated by the off-sites were avant-garde among major U.S. companies at that point in time. At the same time, however, they were altogether aligned with the core philosophies and values of the company throughout its entire history. In this way, the off-site training sessions helped Levi Strauss & Co. reinforce its founding principles:

- Corporate responsibility

- Commitment to addressing select, challenging social issues of the day

- Dedication to attending to the needs and desires of its employees

- Responsibility and support to the communities in which it operated

- Leadership/financial/volunteer support for universities, civic organizations, and national-level social justice and responsibility causes

There are numerous notable examples of Levi Strauss's philosophies and values in action over the years. In the late 1940s, when the company expanded its California facilities, the factories were racially integrated. In the 1960s, it opened such factories in the South. In the 1950s, the company worked with the American Friends Service Committee to distribute jeans to refugees in Korea. In 1968, the Community Affairs Department was founded, and in 1970, the company began Community Involvement Teams, teams of employees who offered volunteer community service—a program that continues today. In 1982, the company promoted AIDS awareness and education in a corporate initiative that was among the first of its kind. In 1991, it was the first multinational company to develop a comprehensive code of conduct to ensure that individuals making its products anywhere in the world would do so in safe and healthy working conditions and be treated with dignity and respect. In 1992, Levi Strauss & Company became the first Fortune 500 company to extend full medical benefits to domestic partners of employees. And, for employees laid off by occasional plant closings, the company provided unusually helpful support to the employees and their communities. In 1992 and 1993, Levi Strauss & Company was among the ten "most admired" U.S. companies, as assessed by *Fortune*, making it the only privately owned company to have been so ranked. It's no wonder, then, that when Levi Strauss died, he was honored by San Francisco as a generous philanthropist who helped San Francisco prosper.

Importantly, as a business enterprise, Levi Strauss & Company thoughtfully tied its core values to its history and experience with an explicit assumption that business can drive profits through principles and that the company's values give it a competitive advantage. The following passage from its "Vision and Values" statement appears on the company's website:

Empathy—walking in other people's shoes

Empathy begins with paying close attention to the world around us. We listen and respond to the needs of our customers, employees, and other stakeholders.

Originality—being authentic and innovative

The pioneering spirit that started in 1873 with the very first pair of blue jeans still permeates all aspects of our business. Through innovative products and practices, we break the mold.

Integrity—doing the right thing

Integrity means doing right by our employees, brands, company, and society as a whole. Ethical conduct and social responsibility characterize our way of doing business.

Courage—standing up for what we believe

It takes courage to be great. Courage is the willingness to tell the truth and to challenge hierarchy, accepted practice, and conventional wisdom. It means standing by our convictions and acting on our beliefs.

We are the embodiment of the energy and events of our time, inspiring people from all walks of life with a pioneering spirit. Generations have worn Levi's® jeans, turning them into a symbol of freedom and self-expression in the face of adversity, challenge, and social change. Our customers forged a new territory called the American West. They fought in wars for peace. They instigated counter-culture revolutions. They tore down the Berlin Wall. Reverent, irreverent—they took a stand.

As evidenced by this portrayal of Levi Strauss & Company's long-standing principled approach to its relationships with its employees and society, two key elements that are inherent in the company's soul become apparent:

1. The dedicated, philanthropic, social-minded philosophies and action orientation of the multi-generational founding family that has guided the company since its founding.[8]

2. The company's extraordinary caring and dedication to the well-being of its employees, communities, and society as a whole.

---

[8] In its 158-year history, the company has had three *non*-family CEOs: Bob Grohman (1981–1984), Phil Marineau (1999–2006), and John Anderson (2007–present).

The remaining three elements of Levi Strauss & Company's soul, cited below, relate to its long and proud business history and to its world-renowned jeans, both of which are vitally intertwined with the development and culture of the American West:

1. Levi's® blue jeans, as captured in the company's "Vision & Values" statement: "Rooted in the rugged American West, Levi's® jeans embody *freedom and individuality*. They are young at heart. *Strong and adaptable*, they have been worn by generations of individuals who have made them their own. They are a symbol of frontier *independence, democratic idealism, social change, and fun* ...."

2. The company's long, rich corporate heritage, including its strong connections to and reflections of the history and culture of the American West

3. The pervading sense of a "family business" that has transcended the company's nearly 160 years in business robustly links the goals, struggles, values, and achievements of each era; and provides great *continuity* and consistency over time. The family is very much the heart of the company.

Today, the company remains *the* world's jeans wear provider, with sales in more than 100 countries.[9]

Williams-Sonoma

In 2007, as part of its fiftieth anniversary celebration[10], Williams-Sonoma, Inc., arguably North America's favorite home furnishings company and specialty retailer, published a small book dedicated to its employees: *50 Years Tells a Story*. Williams-Sonoma, Inc. is an organization that pursues a "People First" philosophy and relies on stories about customers and its associates (that is,

---

[9] Most of the foregoing history of the company was gleaned from Lynn Downey's *Images of America: Levi Strauss & Company* (Arcadia Publishing, 2007); interviews with two company leaders; and Robert Howard's "Values Makes the Company: An Interview with Robert Haas," *Harvard Business Review* (September 16, 1990).

[10] In 1954, Chuck Williams purchased a hardware store in Sonoma, California, and converted it into a store specializing in French cookware. Two years later, he moved his store to San Francisco, where his annual buying trips in France helped Williams develop a unique French cooking and serving equipment center. It was an era in which Julia Child's TV program stimulated new American interest in cooking. In 1986, under the leadership of Howard Lester, who had purchased the company many years earlier with the intention of turning it into an aspirational lifestyle brand, the acquisition was made of the 27-store Pottery Barn brand from the Gap. In 2001, Pottery Barn Kids was launched; in 2002, West Elm was launched; and in 2003, PB Teen was launched.

employees). As such, it was fitting that, in order to promulgate the company's spirit, *50 Years Tells a Story* was a compilation of short remembrances by associates and a few partners (vendors) about Williams-Sonoma, Inc. and its meaning to them.

To exemplify the soul of this admirable, vibrant organization, the following 12 excerpts from *50 Years* indeed tell the Williams-Sonoma, Inc. story:

- "There's nothing better in business—or life—than **exceeding the expectations of people who believed in you** when you were not much more than a dream. The key is finding the right dream and the people who will share it with you." Howard Lester, Chairman and CEO, Williams-Sonoma, Inc.

- "Chuck (Williams) was convinced we could sell ice cream and sorbet through the catalog, if we could figure out how to get them to our customers without melting. We did do it amazingly, one spring … all because Chuck **believed it could be done**." Vice President, Merchandising, Williams-Sonoma Catalog, San Francisco.

- "Chuck and Williams-Sonoma are impossible. They aren't satisfied with just a great knife. No! They want a unique knife, a knife that nobody else has, a knife that is better than best, and a knife that people can afford. **What Chuck wants is just not possible, but we continue to do it**." Wolfgang Wüstof, Chairman, Wüstof family board, Solingen, Germany (knife manufacturer).

- "In the words of Chuck Williams, '**If you love what you do, then the world will fall in love with you**.' I feel privileged to have witnessed this conviction in our associates, our stores, and our company." General Manager, Pottery Barn Bed & Bath, Chelsea, New York.

- "We have all heard the quote, 'It takes a village.' **I believe we are a village at Williams-Sonoma, Inc.** I also believe it started with Chuck, Howard, and Pat (Connolly) many years ago. They continue to set the example for us every day." Director, Direct-to-Customer Operations, Williams-Sonoma, Inc., San Francisco.

- "Whenever I am asked why I have spent 17 years at Williams-Sonoma, Inc., I cheerfully list all the virtues of working for a company that has inspirational leadership, **innovative and exceptional merchandise**, industry-leading catalogs, award-winning retail stores, the best office location in San Francisco, and of course, Chuck Williams. Why would you want to be anywhere else?" Director, Visual Merchandising, Williams-Sonoma Home, San Francisco.

- **"I am working for a company that encourages and celebrates joy and passion in everyday routine!"** District Manager, Pottery Barn, New Jersey District.

- "Work is not just a place, it is like home, because we are not just associates, **we are family.**" Manager, Human Resources, Distribution Center, Memphis, Tennessee.

- **"Our customers often greet us as old friends**. They share with us the events of their lives and are a part of the Williams-Sonoma family. It is that 'family feeling' that makes Williams-Sonoma a special place to work and to shop." Sales Associate, Williams-Sonoma, Marietta, Georgia.

- "No other retailer **values the people in the field** more than this organization." District Manager, South Florida, Williams-Sonoma.

- "It makes me feel proud to be working for **a company that allows me to feel that, yes, I do make a difference in peoples' lives**." Retail Furniture, Customer Service Agent, Customer Care Center, Camp Hill, Pennsylvania.

- "I keep a box on my desk filled with memories from my 10 years here. Inside this box are photos, cards, and funny mementos. Each one reminds me of the **support and encouragement** I have received from my teammates and bosses when my life has brought both joys and heartaches. This company, and the remarkable people who give so much of themselves to it, contribute to who I am. I am proud to work at Williams-Sonoma Inc." Manager, Corporate Finance, Williams-Sonoma, Inc.

As reflected in this assortment of vignettes and mini-testimonials, the soul of this $4 billion company is an amalgam of several factors:

- The inspiration, high standards, great taste, customer-caring devotion, and lessons from its (now 96-year-old) founder, Chuck Williams.

- The inspiration, spirit, and drive of its visionary entrepreneurial leader, Howard Lester, who grew the company in 32 years from a tiny struggling one into an acclaimed national icon. He did so based on entrepreneurial spirit, feelings of ownership among its employees, smart commercial strategy, attention to detail,[11] and tremendous respect, affection, and devotion to company associates in the stores who cared for the customers.

- The companywide family feeling among associates at all levels of the organization who showed respect, admiration, caring, and affection for each other and who encouraged all associates to think of new ideas and to voice them and their suggestions for the betterment of all.

- The associates' love and interest in the home and their devotion to helping customers have beautiful homes[12] and celebrate their homes.

The companies discussed in this chapter bear important similarities to the not-for-profit organizations presented in Chapter 2: they have been vitally concerned about groups of people in society (prospects, clients, and customers) who struggle with challenges and/or unfulfilled aspirations; they have made commitments and have passionately aligned themselves to serving their designated clients; and they have developed and depended on proprietary know-how, capabilities, and philosophies to succeed in their work. Employees have found great meaning in their companies' quests and philosophies; have had considerable self-pride engendered by their organization's purposes, knowledge, and capabilities; and have engaged passionately in their work and that of their organization. Overall, these organizations have consistently sustained high levels of performance.

---

[11] One longtime associate described Howard Lester in this way: "He had the vision of a big picture entrepreneur and the attention to detail of an exceptional craftsman."

[12] In 2010, the company's overarching objective was "to enhance our customers' lives at home." Howard Lester stated his perspective this way: "We are about fun, how to entertain, enjoy cooking, and taste and smell."

Common Traits and the Power of Organizations' Souls

What do the examples of companies and not-for-profit organizations discussed in Chapters 2 and 3 suggest about the nature, ingredients, and power of their souls? Each organization featured, in its own specific way, exemplifies the definition of *soul*, which consists of five principal ingredients that are discussed in depth below.

Ingredient #1: Concerns

Each cited organization has *concerns* about a group of people who need assistance or about a problem in society or a challenge to the world that needs to be addressed and solved. When an organization demonstrates a commitment to addressing such a specific societal need or problem, it does so by providing its services to others who are impacted by the problem, such as homeless youth; poor, sick, homeless, or uneducated individuals;

homeowners; savers; borrowers; investors; retirees; laborers; students; or any of the countless other people in this world who are in need of attention, support and responsiveness.

The concerns for others that these organizations hold strongly touch the hearts of their employees, stirring their emotions, influencing their thinking, calling them to action, and instilling in them a strong sense that they are part of a community of like-minded colleagues who believe that taking action to address the needs of the targeted others is worthwhile, virtuous, admirable, and highly respectable. These organizations' concerns evoke passion, inspiration, commitment, and pride; are galvanizing and uplifting; and stoke employees' desires for engagement.

As mentioned above, concerns can relate to widely *differing* types of people, needs, and problems to be solved. For example, SFO is driven to achieve and provide much more than a financially self-sustaining, safe, and secure landing field. Due to the concern SFO's staff has for representing its home city as positively and distinctively as possible, it strives to ensure that passengers' impressions and memories of San Francisco are as positive as possible. SFO's commitment is to operate an *outstanding* airport that provides world-class service to customers with a distinctive San Francisco style. Dodge & Cox and Merrill Lynch, on the other hand, were each concerned that investors' interests weren't being properly safeguarded by the banks and brokerages that serviced them. BGI was concerned that investors' portfolios weren't afforded the best possible returns and fee structure, while the Stanfords were concerned about the children of California and how California society and its economy would develop. Chuck Williams and Howard Lester were concerned about how Americans could enjoy and enhance their cooking experiences and their homes. Meanwhile, generations of Levi Strauss & Company leaders and employees were concerned about the suitability of clothing used for work and casual occasions by certain trades and then for the general public, as well as being concerned about the well-being of their employees and communities.

Beyond the examples cited thus far, such concerns can also be seen as powerful driving forces in many other organizations. Consider the following two examples, one from the not-for-profit realm, and the other from business. Charlotte Maxwell, a social worker in Oakland, California, who died of ovarian cancer in 1988, was passionately concerned that low-income women should have access to the acupuncture and herbal therapies that helped her in her final months. Her concerns prompted six women to pool $4,000 in 1989 to found what later became the Charlotte Maxwell Complementary Clinic in Oakland, a facility that provides the kinds of care Charlotte Maxwell had envisaged for women without the means to pay for it themselves.[1] Among businesses, Apple, the United States' most valuable company of all time, is a well-publicized example of a company that is driven by a specific concern. Over the years as the company transitioned from a personal computer startup to a world-leading consumer products provider, Apple's principal concerns evolved from individuals who are constrained in their creativity, taste, communications, and control over their lives by the tools available to them to individuals who want a seamless, simple, versatile, and controllable digital lifestyle.

In these examples, the concerns of each organization or their leader(s) at the time, led to thoughtful and sustained *commitments and quests to do something about their concerns.*[2] This brings us to the second ingredient of an organization's soul. ...

Ingredient #2: A Determined Quest/ Commitment to Address the Organization's Concerns

Determined quests and commitments undertaken by organizations to address their concerns are reflected in leaders' calls to action and organizations' rallying cries, reasons for being, and aspirations. As examples:

- Levi Strauss & Company's "Vision & Values" statement, cited earlier

- Oracle: "We will change the way knowledge is amassed and stored."

- Ashoka: "Everyone a changemaker!"

- National Gallery of Art: "Serve the USA in a national role by preserving, collecting, exhibiting, and fostering the understanding of works of art, at the highest possible museum and scholarly standards."

- Intuit: "Revolutionize how people manage their financial lives."

---

[1] Pamela O'Malley Chang, "Fighting the Cancer, Healing the Soul," *Yes!* (Fall 2006), p. 42.

[2] According to Henry Kissinger, "Were history confined to the mechanical repetition of the past, no transformation would ever have occurred. Every great achievement was a vision before it became a reality." "The China Challenge," *Wall Street Journal*, May 14–15, 2011.

- Irish Immigration Center: "Keep hope alive for the many immigrants and their families who turn to us for help."

- SEC: "Protect investors and maintain the integrity of the securities markets."

- Guggenheim Museum (Bilbao, Spain): "Change the fabric of an industrial to a knowledge-based city with a focus on leisure, tourism, and culture."

- MD Anderson Cancer Center, (cited earlier): "Eliminate cancer in Texas, the nation, and the world; be the premier cancer center in the world."

- Facebook: "Give people the power to share and make the world more open and connected."

- Intel: "Creating the building blocks of the Internet economy."

- Bank of America (originally Bank of Italy): A.P. Giannini called out to other San Francisco bankers in the days after the great earthquake and fire of April 1906: "Gentlemen ... if you keep banks closed until November ... there will be no city or people left to serve. Today is the time they need you ... tomorrow morning, I am putting a desk on Washington Street Wharf with a Bank of Italy sign over it. Any man who wants to rebuild San Francisco can come there ... I advise all of you bankers to beg, borrow, or steal a desk and follow my example."[3]

- BGI: "We seek to create financial freedom and security for millions of individuals and thousands of companies around the world."

- Apple: "Provide the tools for individuals' minds to unleash and liberate their power and potential to work differently with additional quality and creativity, and to learn and communicate. Build a company that will invent the future and change the world. Build great products and an enduring great company that is imbued with innovative creativity."

In all of these examples of determined quests and commitments to address concerns and provide benefits to others, employees in these organizations find their organizational determination to be high-minded and inspirational to themselves at the same time that they are meaningful, intrinsically rewarding,

---

[3] Julian Dana, *Giants in the West* (Prentice Hall, 1947, p. 58).

and galvanizing for their overall organizations. Their *commitment* unleashes employees' capabilities, creativity, energies, and wit, as suggested in these moving words in *The Scottish Himalayan Expedition*, and the Genentech example that follows, which is a recent business and science experience that mirrors the wisdom of *The Scottish Himalayan Expedition*:

> *Until one is committed, there is hesitancy, the chance to draw back, always ineffectiveness. Concerning all acts of initiative (and creation), there is one elementary truth, the ignorance of which kills countless ideas and splendid plans: that the moment one definitely commits oneself, then Providence moves too. All sorts of things occur to help one that would never otherwise have occurred. A whole stream of events issues from the decision, raising in one's favour all manner of unforeseen incidents and meetings and material assistance, which no man could have dreamt would have come his way. I have learned a deep respect for one of Goethe's couplets: 'Whatever you can do, or dream you can, begin it. Boldness has genius, power, and magic in it.'[4]*

Dr. Susan Desmond-Hellman, current chancellor of the University of California San Francisco (UCSF) and former executive vice president of development and product operations and chief medical officer of Genentech, credits her former company's rapid success in cancer medicines to a mixture of good science and strategic focus. "Genentech changed from being an organization that did a wide variety of things to being a company that had focus: there was a value added in Genentech's saying that we're going to focus on oncology. That helped promote a new willingness to license drugs from outside the company and prompted a recruiting strategy to attract star players in the cancer field." In 1996, Art Levinson, then-CEO of Genentech, told the sales force that within seven years he expected half of sales to come from cancer drugs. It was a stretch for a company with not a single cancer drug to its name, but Genentech met the goal within four years.

The intensity of feelings that employees develop from their organization's quest and commitment to serve the needs of others or a sector in society, and the extent to which the employees will engage wholeheartedly in working in support of their organization's quest and commitment are usually much stronger than when an organization's purpose or aspirations are principally *self-serving* such as "becoming the largest" or "the most efficient" or "the best-known" or "the highest earning."

---

[4] W.H. Murray, *The Scottish Himalayan Expedition* (J.M. Dent & Sons Ltd., 1951).

Ingredient #3: Understandings

The third element that makes up an organization's soul is the understandings the organization has about how it should best address its concerns. By using the concepts, principles, assumptions, rules of thumb, processes, and practical experience an organization possesses, it can expect to achieve mastery over challenges it will encounter en route to living out its quest and commitment to addressing its concerns. Examples of *understandings* possessed by the organizations cited earlier in the book include Larkin Street's continuum of services, BGI's passive investment approach, Stanford's innovative and entrepreneurial approaches to education and to managing the university over time, Dodge & Cox's long-term investment perspectives and team approach to investing, and the Sisters of Mercy's determination to "go to where the poor are."

These understandings can be incorporated into an organization's strategy; administrative practices; leadership style; culture; values; intellectual property; administrative infrastructure; organization of work; design and creation of its products and services; and/or operating philosophies, as exemplified by the following organizations:

- The underlying values of the U.S. Interagency Council on Homelessness: "(1) Homelessness is unacceptable. (2) There are no homeless people, but rather people who have lost their homes and deserve to be treated with respect. (3) Homelessness is expensive; it is better to invest in solutions. (4) Homelessness is solvable. (5) Homelessness can be prevented. (6) There is strength in collaboration."

- An administrative policy of 3M, the very successful multinational company that is highly dependent on innovation. The policy is intended to reward business units' commercialization of their innovation while ensuring the availability of such innovation to all of 3M's businesses: "Products belong to divisions but technologies belong to the company."[5] This policy is intended to preempt the tendency in many organizations for employees and their business units to be possessive and secretive about their breakthroughs.

- The strategic and cultural philosophy of Citibank's successful wholesale businesses in the 1970s and 1980s:

---

[5] Cited in Sumantra Ghashal and Christopher A. Bartlett, *The Individualized Corporation* (Harper Business, 1997).

- Expansion of size, services offered, and geographical presence

- Being the biggest, best, most innovative, and most profitable firm in existence

- Autonomy and entrepreneurship via decentralization

- Meritocracy

- Aggressiveness and self-confidence

- The operating philosophies and guiding economic principles of Berkshire Hathaway as enunciated by Chairman Warren Buffett to shareholders in 1996 in "An Owner's Manual" (since updated).

- Apple's understandings about designing and delivering compellingly beautiful, simple, clean, user-friendly, and technologically advanced products and services; its user interface; the manner in which it designs, creates, and manages outstanding, unique, and beautiful retail stores;[6] its intense focus on a limited number of products and priorities; its successful cannibalization of its products and services; its obsession with the user's experience; the simple, clear product messaging it employs for breakthrough products; its desire to achieve organizational alignment, a can-do spirit and cooperative work teams; and its flexibility to adjust to new insights and imperatives.

- Nordstrom's performance management (goals, training, review, coaching, rewards) and culture that inspire and motivate high levels of customer service.

- The U.S. Marine Corps' knowledge of how to engender emotional energy and engage the hearts and minds of frontline Marines by

  - Investing heavily in the cultivation of core values

---

[6] As of mid-2011, "More people visit Apple's 326 stores in a single quarter than the 60 million who visited Walt Disney Co.'s four biggest theme parks last year." "Apple's Retail Secrets," *San Francisco Chronicle*, June 15, 2011, pp. A1, 12. As of mid-2012, Apple stores were the most productive in U.S. retail, generating $6,123 revenues per square foot (versus $801 by Best Buy and $135 by JC Penney). Barney Jopson, "Apple Stores Put JC Penney and Best Buy in Shade," *Financial Times*, August 11–12, 2012, p. 10.

- Preparing every individual to lead

- Teaching how high-performance teams operate

- Attending to all individuals' needs

- Building self-discipline[7]

- Pinkus Zuckerman's explanations of the leadership sensitivities and elements he used to guide the renowned St. Paul Chamber Orchestra in its preparation for a concert series:

  - Submerge one's own ego and work for the whole.

  - The joy of excellence for its own sake.

  - The more discipline you have, the more freedom you have.

  - Know where the most important voice is (among the instruments).

  - Pride in the unit.

  - Everyone knows how each performer is doing.

  - Intensity of efforts.

  - An "inexplicable feeling."[8]

- MD Anderson Cancer Center's mission statement, which explains how "cancer will be eliminated: through outstanding programs that integrate patient care, research, and prevention, and through education for undergraduate and graduate students, trainees, professionals, employees, and the public."

An organization's understandings are thus key elements of its soul because they reflect its distinctive qualities, character, know-how, maturation, and operating modes; and as exemplified above, they are incorporated widely into an organizations' strategy, leadership, administrative practices, employment policies, and culture. They are thus important sources of employees' alignment,

---

[7] Jon Katzenbach and Jason Sartamaria, "Firing Up the Front Line," *Harvard Business Review* (May/June 1999), pp. 107-17, 210.
[8] From *Bill Moyers Presents*, (PBS).

confidence, and pride in their organization's competence and potential, and provide vital links between an organization's quest and commitment to pursue its concerns and its ability to succeed.

Ingredient #4: Core Philosophies and Beliefs

The fourth element that makes up an organization's soul is its *core philosophies and beliefs* about what is important, what counts most, and what employee behaviors are appropriate as the organization pursues its objectives. Many of an organization's key philosophies and beliefs are handed down by its founders and leaders and, over time, become the bedrock upon which elements of an organization's leadership and management style, culture, administrative practices, and strategy are built and maintained over time.

All of the organizations featured in this book are deeply influenced by certain beliefs and philosophies they hold about how they should approach their work, how they should provide service to others, and how employees should relate to each other. As reminders of examples that were cited in Chapters 2 and 3:

- Dodge & Cox's mandate that clients' interests come first

- Merrill Lynch's "traditions of trust" vis-à-vis clients and Mother Merrill behavior norms

- Levi Strauss & Company's dedication to its employees' and communities' well-being

- Williams-Sonoma, Inc.'s persistent question of "How would Chuck do it?"

- The Sisters of Mercy's emphasis on hospitality and selflessness

- Larkin Street's openness to all youth

- SFO's belief that each of its employees is responsible for the airport's success

- Wells Fargo's credo that employees are its most important stakeholders.

A few additional illustrations of other highly successful organizations' core philosophies and beliefs add emphasis to their importance in each organization's soul. Consider Northwestern Mutual Life Insurance Company, for example. The 155-year-old company's "The Northwestern Mutual Way," created by its executive committee in 1888, has been used as a credo for more than 100 years. It states, "The ambition of Northwestern has been less to be large than to be safe; its aim is to rank first in benefits to policyholders rather than first in size. Valuing quality above quantity, it has preferred to secure its business under certain salutary restrictions and limitations rather than to write much larger business at the possible sacrifice of these valuable points which have made the Northwestern pre-eminently the policy-owner's company." The company became the first-ever direct provider of life insurance to reach $1 trillion of individual life insurance in force. As a reflection of the esteem in which the company is held, in *Fortune*'s 2011 annual survey, Northwestern Mutual was named the "World's Most Admired Company" in the life insurance industry.

McKinsey & Company is yet another example of a firm that has put its core philosophies and beliefs front and center. The management consulting firm's founder, Marvin Bower, established professional principles for the company's staff: put the client first, practice ethical conduct, maintain client confidentiality, act with competence and candor with clients.[9] Or consider the Ritz-Carlton Hotels' mantra: "We are ladies and gentleman serving ladies and gentlemen." J.P. Morgan, Jr., set forth some of his company's core philosophies and beliefs in 1933, "If I may be permitted to speak of the firm of which I have the honor to be the senior partner: I should state that at all times the idea of doing only first-class business and that in a first-class way, has been before our minds." Similarly, Warren Buffett of Berkshire Hathaway put forth ideals for his firm's long-term management perspectives when he said, "I ask my executives to run the business as if it is the only asset their family has; they can't sell it; and they are going to own it for 100 years."

Timberland, whose CEO, Jeffrey Swartz, strongly supported the employees' and organizations' belief in volunteerism, instituted policies of paid leave for employees desiring to volunteer, sabbaticals to employees who want to volunteer for charitable endeavors, and an annual companywide one-day closure so all employees can participate with one another in community service.[10] Apple included numerous precepts that we can consider to be its core philosophies and beliefs, including the ideas that any individual can change the world; it is imperative to think differently; we are rebels/countercultural; we strive for excellence in all we do; we insist on personal responsibility and accountability; we have endless drive; we expect hard work; we believe in secrecy and security, cooperative spirit, candor, and a sense of urgency; we believe that products are works of art; we employ only "A" players; we are a

---

[9] "Founding Father of Consultancy," *Financial Times*, January 27, 2003.

[10] Elizabeth Schwinn, "Clothing Company CEO Wears Passion for Service on His Sleeve," *The Chronicle of Philanthropy*, January 22, 2004, p. 14.

product company; we know what Steve Jobs considered important. Facebook, meanwhile, kept things simple with its motto: "Move Fast. Break things."

As you can see, an organization's core philosophies and beliefs can have many ways of impacting how an organization operates. J.P. Morgan, Northwestern Mutual, and Ritz-Carlton all use their core philosophies to dictate what strategic path to take and how to conduct business. Warren Buffett and Northwestern Mutual focus on how to view the business and how to manage it. McKinsey & Company, Ritz-Carlton, and J.P. Morgan all try to understand how best to relate to their clients. Ritz-Carlton and McKinsey & Company place an emphasis on how employees should view themselves and act. Perhaps most tellingly, all of the organizations cited are *driven* by what really counts to them.

As such, core philosophies and beliefs set the tone for an organization and serve as guides for decision-making, policies, programs, and processes. Because the output of an organization is the sum of thousands, or even millions, of decisions and activities that are undertaken by its employees, its core philosophies and beliefs are an essential element of its soul, for they help an organization define its character, distinctiveness, and vitality. They also allow the organization to preserve its transcendent qualities and capabilities over time among new employees and, as the organization expands, to new geographies and consumers.

Ingredient #5: Stories about the Beliefs, Hopes, Visions, Principles, Devotion, Insights, and Struggles of Organizations' Founders, Important Leaders, and Contributors

The final element in an organization's soul are stories[11] about founders', important leaders', and contributors' beliefs, hopes, visions, principles, devotion, insights, and struggles. All of the organizations featured as examples in Chapters 2 and 3 ensure that their employees are well aware of their employers' roots, and they do so by instilling founding stories into the culture of their workplaces. As a result, Dodge & Cox employees know about the struggles the firm's founders faced and the core operating approaches and principles they used to build the firm during stressful economic times.

---

[11] "Storytelling is an excellent way of caring for the soul. It helps us see the themes that circle in our lives." Thomas Moore, *Care of the Soul* (Harper Collins, 1992, p. 13).

Employees at BGI are aware of the firm's intellectual pioneering and zeal to change the world of money management. No one at Merrill Lynch could claim to lack knowledge of Charlie Merrill's "Principles," nor would employees at Williams-Sonoma, Inc., forget about Chuck William's taste and customer care or Howard Lester's imaginative business approaches and respect for associates. Levi Strauss & Company employees share a common respect for the concern that Levi Strauss, the Sterns, and the Haas family members had for employees, social justice, and society. All new Sisters of Mercy learn about founder Mother McAuley's selfless, courageous, and generous dedication to the poor. Larkin Street employees and board members never forget the not-for-profit's founding belief that homeless and at-risk youth could be saved. Faculty, staff, students, and alumni at Stanford University respect the Stanfords' dedication to building a great university. Similarly, the individuals that make up the Notre Dame family resonate with the university founder's quest to "do good." And what about SFO Director John Martin's vigilance and high standards? They are embodied by SFO employees every day.

Stories from an organization's past can provide inspiration, grounding, and connection for employees as well as bases for courage, hope, and high standards. Stories about an organization's founders, important leaders, and major figures can contribute substantially to the transcendence and intensity of the organization's life force, inner character, and essential spirit. Why? Because stories are a principal means of informing, illustrating, and reminding employees what is important and special about their organization, how it became what it is, and how current employees can be good stewards of the organization and safeguard its future.

An example of the use of stories was cited in the *Financial Times* on January 12, 2010: "When David Booth, chief executive of Dimensional Fund Advisors, was looking for ways to make recent recruits feel part of the business that he co-founded in 1981, he thought of producing a company history. So he rounded up members of the original team and got them to talk on camera about their early memories of pioneering investment products. 'The written word is great,' says Mr. Booth. 'But seeing and hearing people makes you feel a personal connection.'"

Apple, like Booth, understands the important impact that founding stories can have on its workplace. As such, stories abound at Apple about Steve Jobs's vision, genius, strong will, impatience, persistence, and brashness. Accounts of the company's founding, early struggles, successful products, and key decisions (such as to open retail stores and to switch to Intel microprocessors) also proliferate. Steve Jobs's rescue and turnaround of the company is another common topic of conversation, and anecdotes about certain individuals who were of immense importance to the company at various junctures in its development flourish. In fact, Jobs so strongly believed in the power of stories and examples to further build and solidify Apple's culture that he created Apple University and commissioned the writing of Apple case studies that could transmit the company's history and culture to new generations of employees.

There are countless ways for an organization to impart its stories to its employees and the larger world as Land Rover demonstrated in the May 20, 2011, issue of *The Wall Street Journal*. In a full-page advertisement, which featured a portrait of a company legend and several blocks of descriptive text, Land Rover detailed a story about a very important organizational contributor: "It was 1945, World War II's aftermath found Great Britain both economically depressed and in the midst of a crippling steel shortage ... the assembly lines at Rover Car Company were now at a complete standstill until a miracle could save the company from financial collapse. And a miracle was just what happened when Rover Company engineer and eccentric thinker Maurice Wilks hit on a stroke of genius. A notion so bold and audacious that it would single-handedly revolutionize automotive design ... Maurice Wilks' idea was to build a simple four-wheel-drive vehicle that could master any type of terrain. Something along the lines of the then-popular military-issue Jeep. Only instead of using a traditional stamped steel body, Rover would use aluminum alloy, three times more costly than steel, yet readily accessible in Great Britain ... its extensive use of aluminum ... highly resistant to rust ... would better handle and negotiate steep inclines ... to this day, Land Rover continues to embrace Maurice Wilks' visionary thinking by utilizing aluminum alloy throughout the design of its vehicle."

No matter the manner in which they are relayed, *stories* are an ingredient in an organization's soul in that they provide explanations for the organization's approaches and standards, contribute to the organization's sense of coherence, and engender feelings of interest, pride, loyalty, affiliation, commitment, grounding, confidence, identification, and inspiration. Stories connect employees to their organization's founding, founders, early struggles, and to other employees. They are therefore an essential element in an organization's soul.

For ease of reference, the following Tables 4-1, 4-2, and 4-3 summarize the eleven featured organizations' souls.

Table 4-1. Summary of the Souls of the 11 Example Organizations—Not-for-Profits

	Sisters of Mercy	**Larkin Street Youth Services**	**University of Notre Dame**	**Stanford University**
Concerns for people/problems to be solved involving service to others	Welfare of the poor, especially women and children	Welfare of homeless youth	Anyone constrained by poverty, injustice, or oppression from pursuing their dreams Catholic place of quality higher education	The great issues of the day Quality education
Determined **quest/ commitment** to address concerns	Be with the poor and help them develop self-sufficiency	Get kids off the streets for good Never give up	Quality education, open inquiry, and community to forge concern and commit-ment to common good	Render the highest possible service to mankind as a university in support of a better future for subsequent generations Maintain the highest standards of teaching, research, and athletics
Understandings of how to address concerns	Go where the poor are Be close to the poor Connect the wealthy with the poor	Homeless youth are vulnerable but resilient Need a continuum of services and a team effort	Strong sense of community Engagement with society about issues of the day Distinctive Catholic university	Importance of entrepreneurship, innovation, pioneering spirit Bringing together outstanding students, scholars, and teachers Facilitated by "The Farm"

Philosophies and beliefs: What matters most	A call from God\n\nLifelong devotion to works of mercy\n\nLife in religious community	All youth deserve a chance to reach their potential	Provide a beacon for and symbol of the American Dream\n\nHigher purpose through service\n\nPursuit of academic and athletic excellence	Standard of excellence\n\nValue of quality education\n\nContributing to knowledge and society in important ways
Stories about origins and leaders (founders, original mission/purpose)	Inspired by founder's beliefs and acts of mercy, as well as other Sisters' heroic devotion and acts	Organization born out of neighborhood concern	Catholic belief in the importance of service	Founders' desire to be progressive and create important new university\n\n"The Farm" origins

Table 4-2. Summary of the Souls of the 11 Example Organizations—Public Sector

	SFO
Concerns for people/ problems to be solved involving service to others	Customers', airlines', and communities' air travel requirements
Determined **quest/ commitment** to address concerns	Distinctive services and facilities that reflect San Francisco\n\nSatisfy customers
Understandings of how to address concerns	Very high aspirations\n\nConsistency and reliability in delivery
Philosophies and beliefs: What matters most	Everyone is responsible\n\nConsistency in performance\n\nHighest standards
Stories about origins and leaders (founders, original mission/purpose)	Director's extensive knowledge, high standards, continual push for improvement\n\nCreate beautiful and distinctive terminals

Table 4-3. Summary of the Souls of the 11 Example Organizations—Businesses

	Dodge & Cox	Wells Fargo	Williams-Sonoma, Inc.
Concerns for people/problems to be solved involving service to others	Clients need quality investment advice and support	Customers need quality, convenient banking services	Entertain and celebrate in customers' beautiful and happy homes
Determined quest/ commitment to address concerns	Quality, consistency in long-term relationships	Client- and employee-focused banking services	Lifestyle choices with distinctiveness, beauty, quality, and excellence in shopping experience and service
Understandings of how to address concerns	Maintain long-term perspective Utilize bottoms-up research Engage large numbers of opinions Use team approach to decision-making	Employees are the lynchpin Broad-based distribution system	Bring a sense of joy and celebration into people's lives Offer awareness, education, demonstration, advice, and accessibility Strong sense of family and employee ownership
Philosophies and beliefs: What matters most	Clients' interests come first Remain independent Cautious, conservative approaches	Business must be grounded in vision and values Employees are the most important stakeholders	People first Love what you do Create distinctive products and shopping experience
Stories about origins and leaders (founders, original mission/ purpose)	Founders' vision and struggles Upholding principles over long time period	Stagecoach as trusted channel for assets and transactions	Inspiration and respect for legendary founder and leader

	Barclays Global Investors	Merrill Lynch	Levi Strauss & Co.
Concerns for people/problems to be solved involving service to others	Individuals and organizations around the world want financial security through saving and investment	Clients' financial interests and needs for brokerage services	Casual clothing requirements of populace Social issues of the day Employees' needs
Determined quest/ commitment to address concerns	Convince, then serve investors with superior approach	Care for clients and employees	Develop attractive products and stimulate demand Protect welfare of employees and community
Understandings of how to address concerns	Financial concepts as basis for better returns, less risk, and less expensive way to manage money	Create meritocracy Encourage spirit of underdog/maverick/ performance Create caring, supportive environment Train employees and recognize achievements	Leadership role in community; role model corporate behaviors Continuity of family-run business
Philosophies and beliefs: What matters most	Change the world of investment management to provide improved long-term financial performance	Commitment to clients is more important than advisors' background/ schooling Mother Merrill: We're a family Value integrity, respect for individuals, hard work	Corporate responsibility to employees and community Quality and distinctive products
Stories about origins and leaders (fouders, original mission/ purpose)	Pioneering vision and courageous commitment of founders Firm's successes in influencing industry and the world	Charlie Merrill's Principles CEOs' humble origins and rise to top Hard work pays off	Heritage of American West Levi Strauss as inventor of blue jeans Family values orientation

What Is the Power Exuded by Organizations' Souls?

Strong organizational souls will evoke passionate commitment, great pride, satisfaction, and meaning among its members.[12] They also will inspire in employees feelings of the uniqueness of their employer and the sense that they share a distinctive identity and common cause with their colleagues. In other words, employees of the 11 organizations featured are exceedingly proud of and motivated by the ingredients in their organizations' souls and are inspired by what their organization is and does. They identify with the founding stories of their organization and its early leaders' pioneering spirit, aspirations, struggles, and courage to overcome serious challenges.[13] They feel as though they are a part of their organization's serious and admirable purpose, which is uplifting, compelling, and a source of vitality. (In the words of Sister of Mercy Marilyn Lacey, "It is challenging to maintain freshness of spirit. Our Sisterhood's soul provides us each with energy and light.") They hold fast to the longevity of their organization's principles, purposes, and values. They respect the way their organization approaches its work: with high standards, with its heart as well as its head, with concerns for its clients' best interests always prominent, and with deep concerns for its employees. And, they take pride in their organization's contributions to its clients and to society.

They are also proud of themselves through the association, identity, and influence the organization has on them as individuals. Apple is an excellent example. Reportedly, its employees take pride in the company's products, in the organization's world-leading capabilities, in their founder, whom they considered to be a genius who changed the world, and in themselves as part of Steve Jobs's organization and the Apple story. They feel an affinity with other employees through shared philosophies and beliefs. They have been able to rely on their colleagues with whom they shared a connection to their organization's soul and have been motivated to work collaboratively with them to fulfill their organization's goals and quests. They felt engaged,

---

[12] "Great leaders, like great companies and countries, create meaning, not just money. The values and interests of freedom, self-actualization, learning, community, excellence, uniqueness, service, and social responsibility are the ones that truly attract followers to a common cause." Barry Posner, Jim Kouzes, *The Leadership Challenge*, 4th edition (Jossey-Bass, 2007, p. 116).

[13] "A sense of continuity and history is a powerful way of creating meaning … people yearn to place their activities in some sort of context." Gurnek Bains et al., *Meaning Inc.*, (Profile Books, 2007, p. 84).

energized, and hopeful[14] due to both their desire to faithfully live out their organization's proud destiny and their sense of joining with talented, like-minded peers in pursuing what they believe in.

What Could a Soulless Organization Look Like?

What could an organization without a soul look like? What may come to mind are companies that do something illegal (such as Enron) or make products that are harmful to customers' health. But a company without a soul may be doing neither of these things. It may have an entirely legal business and cause no harm with its products. Its soullessness may simply be the result of an absence of any of the five elements of soul. Maybe it lacks a concern for the welfare of any group outside its executives and shareholders. Maybe it takes only a transactional view of its relationships with its customers and employees.

A prime example of a soulless organization is a technology company that became a household name in the early days of the Internet. The company grew its customer base to 20 million subscribers in a few short years and became the dominant player in its arena. Its consumer business grew based on its ease of use (not common in its category at the time), but as advertisers clamored to get on board, the company abandoned its attention to and sacrificed the quality of its users' experience for the sake of having more to sell to advertisers. The company became infamous for making it almost impossible for subscribers to unsubscribe. Many tried and subsequently gave up.

Advertisers became the next victims. As demand for the company's advertising space grew, the company "believed it could hold advertisers hostage," as one former company executive put it. "The arrogance was off the charts. Their attitude was, 'We're the only game in town, so you'll buy what we're willing to sell you, and you'll be lucky to get it.' The company was so hungry to sell as much as they could that they sold vaporware—things not ready for primetime." While the founder was a visionary whose dream was to take the Internet to the next level, he hired a different breed of people as his lieutenants—highly aggressive salespeople whose vision was solely of dollar signs. As the former executive put it, "The founder had spent ten years unsuccessfully trying to

---

[14] "Students of the American Westward movement are familiar with the powerful sense of the future that characterized so many of the pioneers, the belief that they were part of an immensely exciting drama just begun ... energy is released by self-images of growth and forward movement." John W. Gardner, "The Tasks of Leadership," *Leadership Paper 2*, Independent Sector, March 1986, p. 11.

monetize his vision. He became impatient and brought in people he knew could get it done. When the stock split multiple times in the first 36 months, he looked the other way from his lieutenants' philosophies and business practices."

The company's core beliefs about what is important, what constitutes success, and what behaviors are appropriate were completely focused on money. "It was all about closing deals and raising the stock price. There was no sense of ethics or of building relationships. The reigning philosophy was, 'The end justifies the means,'" said the former executive. "It was like *Glengarry Glen Ross*: people were expected to overachieve and hit their numbers every month (there wasn't much patience for under-delivery!), and in return they got a great facility to work in (the organization built a plush new corporate headquarters), a sexy, high-cachet brand to be associated with, and lots of money. The contract with employees did not include even nourishing your career, let alone your soul."

Organizations such as these, which lack every element of soul and have concern only for their own profits, will attract employees who are guns for hire. These individuals will give no more effort than that which they're paid to give and will leave when there's an opportunity elsewhere for more money or more meaning. While employed, they are unlikely to be advocates for their organizations, and their pride in their employment (if any) will be commensurate with the organization's financial success. In short, they will be unlikely to stick with the company through tough times.

Summary

The soul of an organization has five essential elements that are intertwined:

1. Concerns about a group of people who need help or a societal problem that needs to be solved. These concerns engage employees' emotions and engender in them a desire to help.

2. A determined quest and commitment to address the organization's concerns.

3. Understandings about how to address the organization's concerns. These understandings consist of unique insights and proprietary know-how that the organization has about how it can successfully meet the challenges that stand in the way of helping the target group.

4. Philosophies and beliefs about what is important and how to operate.

5. Stories about the hopes, dreams, values, philosophies, standards, and struggles of the organization's founders, important leaders, and contributors.

When these five elements of soul are present and active in an organization, the organization has a self-generating power to motivate, engage, and inspire employees. Importantly, this power does not wax and wane in direct relationship to the financial ups and downs of the organization. By contrast, a soulless organization must generate a constant supply of carrots (or sticks) to keep the organization moving forward.

Why Organizations Can Endure for Decades

Why do the 11 organizations discussed throughout this book *continue* to have such strong souls a long time after they were founded? How have these organizations' souls managed to transcend decades, transitions in leadership, and the strategic and managerial adaptations necessary to keep up with the demands of changing times? In this chapter, we will explore these questions and more.

Sisters of Mercy

Since their founding in 1831, the Sisters of Mercy have extended their charism (that is, the guiding spirit that energizes their mission) and their work on behalf of the poor across no fewer than 47 countries. The Sisters began by caring for vulnerable women in Dublin, then they practiced nursing alongside Florence Nightingale during the Crimean War, and later they cared for the wounded on both sides of the U.S. Civil War. In the Sisters' archives, they even have a handwritten note from Abraham Lincoln advising that they should be given whatever provisions they might need to continue their work. They moved with immigrant populations to the uncharted American West and to the outback of Australia. They started schools, hospitals, retreat centers, and centers for social justice. Today they work in prison ministry, AIDS relief, adult education, and dementia care; they serve in inner-city schools and in Ivy League universities, in the slums of Soweto and the hollows of Appalachia. They perform all of this service for the simple reason that they feel a calling to assist society's less fortunate members.

To meet emerging needs in society over the past 30 years, the Sisters have founded a number of diverse organizations such as Mercy Housing, which provides affordable housing for the poor throughout the United States; Mercy Center, which serves as a contemplative oasis in the San Francisco Bay Area for retreats and conferences; and Mercy Beyond Borders, whose goal is to improve the lives and prospects of displaced women and girls in South Sudan and Haiti. Always the Sisters desire to work among the poor and to connect the wealthy with the poor.

What enables the Sisters to retain their original spirit, which spans so many generations and cultures—from Papua New Guinea to Peru, from Ireland to Argentina, from Australia to South Africa? One reason is that the organization maintains a strong initiation period for new members, during which there is considerable discernment by both the organization and the individual as to whether the potential new member is a good fit for the organization and if she possesses the charism, (the gift of mercy) that the Sisters so wholly embody. Women who wish to join the Sisters of Mercy are required to journey through a lengthy orientation and "incubation" period for novices, with ample devotion to quietude, prayer, and reflection. They also must attend conferences with veteran mentors, such as Sister Mary Ann Scofield, who mentored hundreds of sisters in a devoted 50-year career. New members hear stories about the founder's life and her good works, and they study the founder's letters and the virtues she personified. They also discuss the Sisterhood's mission, constitution, governance, and way of life; work alongside experienced Sisters to learn what they do and how they live their lives; accompany Sisters on visits to the sick and suffering; and ultimately feel "the spirit, passion, and fire of the Sisters as contemplatives in (concrete) action, responding to the cry of the poor."[1]

Another reason that the Sisters of Mercy are able to keep their original spirit alive is that, in the years that follow their initial five-year incorporation, Sisters of Mercy have periodic one-on-one meetings with dedicated mentors. They also participate in occasional group retreats, meet regularly with their peers, and attend annual retreats. These activities are intended to support their individual needs for reflection, prayer, and renewal; help them keep their spirit

---

[1] As described to the author by Sister Mary Ann Scofield of Burlingame, California.

alive; and ensure that they have a firm foundation before they take their vows. Available to new Sisters is a small book, *Reflection on Ministry*, which contains a series of provocative questions that prompt reflection and greater clarity about their commitment, orientation, mindset, motivation, and activities. They have opportunities to share their perspectives with others with whom they feel close, and over time they are able to share their thoughts with the larger group of nuns in their community.

Over their long careers, Sisters engage in daily meditation, periodic silent reflective retreats, monthly meetings with their spiritual director, and community celebrations of various Sisters' lives and good works. There is much retelling of stories about their founder, which helps the Sisters "avoid Mission creep," reminds them of what is important, and offers them insight into how to approach contemporary issues. They also have various opportunities to learn about and become inspired by other Sisters' current activities and approaches to supporting the poor. For example, the Sisters publish a weekly newsletter that highlights the work of individuals within the organization, and they also attend semiannual, day-long regional Sisters of Mercy gatherings, where Sisters from different regional communities can learn of their leaders' concerns and involvements; discuss issues of common concern; and express their interests in starting new projects in response to newly perceived needs of the poor. (Currently, nuns with a calling to begin an initiative on behalf of the poor are likely to receive permission to try to make it succeed.) Every six years, a Sisters of Mercy congress is held to discuss desirable areas for the Sisterhood's focus (for example, the environment). The congress is made up of elected delegates, but any member can propose topics for discussion and any Sister can attend.

Considering the foregoing description of the Sisters of Mercy, we can now highlight the important contributors that have nourished the organization's soul and kept it strong over the centuries and the wide geographical spread of its members. A lengthy indoctrination and on-boarding process for new members provides ample opportunities to learn the Sisterhood's history, guiding principles, mission, and approaches to doing its work. Thus, each new member becomes a carrier of the core elements of the organization's soul. Stories about its founder as well as the good works of past and present-day Sisters are told and retold with passionate admiration in the Sisterhood's literature, periodicals, and many forums, thereby reminding, inspiring, and aligning the Sisters with what counts most to their organization. Finally, the can-do spirit of the Sisterhood encourages and supports its members when they suggest new initiatives that will address the needs of the poor—thereby providing opportunities for the Sisters throughout their careers to engage in activities that are reflections of their Sisterhood's soul.

Williams-Sonoma

Williams-Sonoma's strong soul has been nourished over the firm's 55 years through the words and deeds of its revered founder, Chuck Williams, and its much-admired business builder, Howard Lester. It is the example and wisdom of these two men that has inspired present-day Williams-Sonoma employees to continuously live and celebrate the Williams-Sonoma "family feeling."

Whenever Williams-Sonoma associates want to generate insights and guidance about the best ways to serve their customers and the most effective methods for creating and selecting distinctive, high-quality products and services for their customers' homes, they ask a simple question: "What would Chuck do?" Chuck Williams has been an icon for the Williams-Sonoma associates. He is beloved, respected, and trusted. He has spoken inspirationally at annual Williams-Sonoma conferences for store associates. His vision for Williams-Sonoma's publishing program prompted him to imaginatively and diligently review more than 12,000 recipes for the company's cookbooks. Largely, as a result of his devoted work, Williams-Sonoma has released 250 cookbook titles, which collectively have sold more than 29 million copies in the past 19 years. And at age 96, Williams is still coming into the office every day to review new recipes. In this way, he continues to exemplify his passion for sharing the pleasures of cooking that have defined the company he founded in 1977.

Howard Lester, the other man behind Williams-Sonoma's resilient soul, built the company from one brand with four stores and $4 million in annual revenues after purchasing it from Williams in 1978. As Pat Connolly, chief marketing officer who was Lester's second hire in 1979, recalls, "Howard was larger than life; he had an amazing presence. He was a natural leader all of his life. He was a courageous decision maker. He was fearless in business. He was very street smart. He could read people. Only once in 30 years did Howard display his ego! He always took the blame, and never the credit personally. He always spoke in terms of 'we.'" Lester also imbued an entrepreneurial spirit by finding individuals who could build businesses. Lester once said, "The key is finding the right dream and finding the people who will share it with you." When he found those people who wanted to share his dream with him, he pushed them to do their best and protected them when mistakes were made or results were slow to materialize. When Lester, Williams, and various associates traveled the world in search of vendors and products, the trips had distinctive pioneering and entrepreneurial qualities.

Lester built a merchant culture around Williams as an icon, and he displayed intense respect, appreciation, and affection for the associates who worked in Williams-Sonoma stores across North America. Year after year, Lester made numerous visits to the stores,[2] conversing with associates and store managers on store floors and in stockrooms. He held town hall meetings for associates wherever he went. He listened intently, eliciting the associates' ideas on how to serve customers better, the types of products that would be most appreciated, how the head office could better support the stores, what was working or not at the store level, and what mistakes the head office was making. Lester firmly believed that "answers to all company questions reside in the knowledge possessed by thousands of associates who work in the stores," and he and Williams repeatedly told associates, "It's *always* about the customers!"

Associates knew that their feedback and ideas were highly valued, so they gave them freely. On store visits, Lester also read customers' appreciation letters, shared his business philosophies, made many practical suggestions, commended associates publicly for their outstanding efforts and achievements, commiserated with them when times were tough or headquarters screwed up, and pushed them to come up with new ideas and visions about what could be. He even discreetly helped associates with serious personal problems. When the Loma Prieta earthquake occurred in 1989, for example, Lester personally saw to it that all associates who lost their homes had a place to live, and he paid for the housing.

Over the years, the store associates grew to revere and trust Lester, so much so that, as Connolly explains, "the field associates would walk across hot coals for Howard." The organization was galvanized and inspired by him and by the company's dedication to their customers and their homes, and associates became very loyal to the company.[3] "They connected to something bigger than their paychecks, and viewed it as their company," explained Laura Alber, the current CEO. "This spirit leads store associates and call center representatives to serve customers as if they were home decorators." Added Sharon McCollam, the company's COO and CFO who retired in 2012, "Williams-Sonoma is alive. It is a 'family' of associates who are passionate about making people happy in their homes. And that passion comes from the

---

[2] Lester's philosophy as reflected in his words: "I think an enterprise is a lot like a rose garden ... a commitment that never ends ... there must be a chain of unbroken loyalty to keep the garden healthy and beautiful. If neglected or taken for granted, a rose garden or enterprise will wither and lose its vitality. Perhaps a rose garden is such a special thing because it speaks to an enduring faith in the importance of investing in tomorrow. That gardening clone today is a worthwhile investment, because the best days for your garden or your company lie ahead."

[3] In the words of Richard Harvey, whose career at the company began as a mailroom clerk and who is now the president of the Williams-Sonoma (kitchen store) brand, "The long tenure here of so many people says it better than anything else could: Howard Lester's legacy is not the company; it is each of us."

'emotional threads' that Howard wove into the culture for more than 30 years." The long tenure of many senior-level executives over the years afforded the organization a lengthy time period in which its core beliefs, guiding spirit, founders' stories, and spirit could take root and flourish in the hearts and minds of its associates. "Many of us in senior positions have been here for a long time," explained Alber, "and we have been shepherds of this culture for many years. It is natural for us to continue and strengthen it."

Before purchasing Williams-Sonoma from Williams in 1978, Lester once jotted down several guiding principles that he believed to be important in business. Many years later, after his wife Mary happened across that list, Lester decided to recite the principles to associates at a companywide conference. The associates were very touched and impressed by "Howard's Rules" (as they came to be called) and, on their own volition, posted them on store and office walls across North America. Today, the company's guiding principles are known, loved, followed, and referred to by associates everywhere. Associates understand that Howard's Rules were the standard by which Lester ran his business, his friendships, and his life.

HOWARD'S RULES

Our Guiding Principles

"Over twenty years ago I took pen to paper and captured the essence of what I had learned and believe are some fundamental principles of business. A few years ago I was asked to deliver a speech. I went back and revisited my faded yellow pad."

1. Without vision it is very difficult, if not impossible, to provide leadership to a company of any size. Dreams are important, never stop having them.

2. Arrogance is a terrible thing. Do not confuse competence and confidence with being arrogant. Arrogant people are unable to understand their own shortcomings and therefore don't work to improve.

3. Be self-critical. The best leaders are always focused on improving. They know what is missing and are fanatical about making corrections.

4. Revere and celebrate your associates and their accomplishments. Remember, they did the work, not you. You may have thought of what needed to be done and provided the leadership, but they did the work

and are proud of the accomplishment. Give them the credit.

5. Integrity and honesty in everything you do set the standards and example for all around you and create the culture of an organization.

6. Always judge your performance by how your customer judges you. Customer metrics are far more important than company metrics. Without customers, nothing else matters.

7. Be continually focused on what can be rather than what is. We either lead or follow. It is better to go where no one has gone than where many have been before.

Each summer, Williams-Sonoma holds a stores conference for about 1,000 North American associates. In addition to revealing the company's business results and prospects and exhibiting the next year's merchandise, the conferences have featured inspirational speeches by Lester, Williams, and other company executives who have reminded the audience of Williams-Sonoma's origins, values, and long-standing philosophies. Featured, too, have been customers' letters of appreciation, moving stories about associates' devotion to their customers' satisfaction and to other associates, and warm-hearted remembrances about Williams and Lester. Recognition is given and honors—notably the People First Award and the Catch the Spirit Award—are presented to selected associates who epitomize what the company stands for and, since 2009, the Howard Lester Award is given to the associate who best embodies the values described in Howard's Rules. Throughout the year, associates look forward to the conference because it gives them the opportunity to emotionally reconnect with their peers, embrace one another warmly, cry and laugh together at inspirational speeches and touching stories, and feel strongly bonded by a shared sense of family. Connolly attests to the care with which the annual conferences are executed: "Hundreds of associates put their souls into producing it; all speakers prepare ten times more than for normal speeches."

"Soon after I was selected by the board as chief executive, Chuck Williams asked me 'What are you going to do?'" explained Alber. "'What do you want me to do?' I asked him. Chuck replied, 'I don't want you to change it, just make it better.'" At the time of Lester's passing in late 2010, Williams-Sonoma employed 20,000 associates; had 600 stores; and had earned almost $4 billion in revenues from six distinct merchandise brands: Williams-Sonoma, Pottery Barn, West Elm, Pottery Barn Kids, PB Teen, and Williams-Sonoma Home. It was alone among public companies as being home-centric and relatively unique among all large companies as a multi-brand, multi-channel business.

Considering what has been related so far about Williams-Sonoma, it is clear that the company has a strong and robust soul principally because its founder, Chuck Williams, and its builder, Howard Lester, lived, exemplified, and spoke frequently about what mattered most to the company. Endearing stories have been told and retold throughout the organization about the company's founding and development as well as about associates' admirable service to customers. Lester, through his extensive travels to the company's stores and back-office installations, had personal contact with associates and embodied the company's soul. And Howard's Rules, which are posted on office and store walls, are a constant reminder of what Lester believed to be important. Many of the recent and current company executives have spent most of their careers at Williams-Sonoma and have been known to be strong believers in the organization's soul. As such, they have modeled its core elements and promulgated the soul wherever they go in the organization and at special forums, such as the stores conference, which is packed with emotion, affection, and passion—all of which reflect the Williams-Sonoma soul.

Wells Fargo Bank

Wells Fargo's soul consists of the core belief that employees are the most important stakeholder and principal source of its competitive advantage; the written "Vision and Values" explanation of the company's most important aspirations, its business model and strategy, its core values and organizational culture; and its 100-year-old stagecoach icon. Its soul has been nourished and reinforced over the years by these four principal means.

The stagecoach icon is used in virtually all of the firm's advertising and graphic displays, and it is a central artifact in Wells Fargo museums and historical presentations. The stagecoach, one of America's best-known and most revered icons, engenders pride, identity, awareness of the company's long and proud history, and a collective sense of "we can make it happen" among employees.

All of the company's strategies, policies, major decisions, and management and administrative practices are in lockstep with its "Vision and Values" statement and are therefore supportive, reflective, and aligned with the core belief that employees are Wells Fargo's most important stakeholders. A senior vice president explained, "I like most how well the bank treats employees. We are encouraged to have a balanced life. There are gender and racial diversity balances and everyone feels accepted. We can dress as we wish. There are ample training and mentoring opportunities to bring individuals up to their full potential. We are encouraged and supported to volunteer for community causes and to assume leadership roles. Employees remain at Wells for a long time, team well with others, and are very engaged!" Another staff specialist related, "When my mom died, both my manager and my human resources liaison said, 'Take as much time as you need. ... We'll take care of you.' When I was feeling kind of guilty about taking a lengthy leave, I said I hoped they had granted me an *unpaid* leave. They responded, 'Don't worry about it. It's all been *paid* leave.' So, I feel renewed loyalty to my company, just as I did following my extensive maternity leave."

The "Vision and Values" document, distributed to all new employees, is reviewed every two years and then distributed to all employees with accompanying town hall meetings, executive speeches, and articles in Wells Fargo periodicals that stress and reconfirm why the bank's core beliefs are good for all stakeholders. "Over the years, the 'Vision and Values' document has been updated to embrace changes in our industry and our business. But the *core* of 'Vision and Values' has remained relatively *constant* since they were first published nearly 25 years earlier," explained Richard Kovacevich, Wells Fargo's CEO at the time of the merger and the principal architect and builder of the current Wells Fargo. No acquisitions are made unless the culture of the firm to be acquired is deemed to be compatible with Wells Fargo's culture. Similarly, no leaders are appointed within Wells Fargo unless they genuinely embrace the bank's vision and values.

Merrill Lynch

In its huge[4] private client business, Merrill Lynch's soul was comprised of both long-standing, "sacred" Principles from founder Charlie Merrill and the firm's Mother Merrill organizational culture. Merrill Lynch's soul transcended the 60 years from 1941 to 2001 for three principal reasons. First, its leaders, most of whom grew up in the firm's private client business and came from working class Irish Catholic families, personally identified with and strongly espoused the firm's guiding principles and its Mother Merrill culture. Second, Mother Merrill was highly appealing to the private client employees and instilled in them the belief that Merrill Lynch was a meritocratic, paternalistic, apolitical, patriotic, inclusive, and fun organization.

Finally, the organization created many venues, platforms, and occasions at which groups of employees came together to honor and celebrate the firm's founders and discuss the traits of its heroes and legends. At these events, the

---

[4] In 2011, Merrill Lynch had approximately 15,000 financial advisors and more than $2 trillion in client assets, making it the world's largest brokerage.

firm retold stories about its two founders, who met at a New York YMCA to discuss the early vision for the firm and its sacred principles of putting the client first and giving one's all to the firm. It also honored current employees who lived by the firm's principles and made notable achievements. And to top things off, employees heard personal reminiscences by CEOs or references to them made by others about the leader's modest upbringing, how these individuals were touched and well-treated by Merrill Lynch when they were young and unknown employees, and how they had worked their way up in the organization. Thus, the organization utilizes spoken history and storytelling about its role models to inspire, educate, reinforce, and galvanize its employees, and as a result, the firm's soul is strengthened.

Levi Strauss & Company

That Levi Strauss & Company's soul has remained strong nearly 160 years after its founding is largely a reflection of two things: the continuity of the founding family as its leaders and the consistency among generations of founding family members in their high-minded social consciousness, genuine caring for their employees and for society, and will to practice their values. The company's soul has also been kept alive and nourished over the years by the respect that the public and employees have shown to both the company and the many generations of its founding family members for their progressive, courageous, and philanthropic civic leadership. The enthusiasm with which so many of its employees engage in company-sponsored community volunteerism plays an important role in preserving Levi Strauss & Company's soul as well, as does the marketplace's validation of its core jeans product.

In the past 30 years, company practices, such as the extensive use of small employee advisory groups, have also reflected and nourished the organization's soul. Leaders have used these advisory groups (usually governance groups, such as the Senior Management Group, Global Leadership Team, and Worldwide Leadership Team) to deliberate about and forge companywide aspirations,[5] missions, and values, as well as to resolve employee issues and highlight employee concerns. An important example was cited earlier: in the late 1980s, CEO Robert Haas instigated three interrelated courses to help leaders and managers fully understand the company's important meanings— the kinds of value-laden behaviors that would be expected of employees—

---

[5] For years, the company derived inspiration, guidance, and positive provocation from its aspirations statement: "We want a company that our people are proud of and committed to, where all employees have an opportunity to contribute, learn, grow, and advance based on merit, not politics or background. We want our people to feel respected, treated fairly, listened to, and involved. Above all, we want satisfaction from accomplishments and friendships, balanced personal and professional lives, and to have fun in our endeavors."

and to encourage the formation of employee affinity groups to discuss workplace issues. Notably, one-third of managers' bonuses was tied to their implementation of company values.

On a related note, in recent decades company leadership has communicated extensively to the entire company what it stands for by retelling colorful and meaningful stories about the company's history and making known the extensiveness of employees' volunteerism. These communications occur in company training classes, new employees' on-boarding sessions, leaders' talks to employee groups, company brochures and booklets, the company website, and in a stirring and colorful historical museum of Levi Strauss & Company's artifacts, which is located in the company's San Francisco global corporate headquarters.

Larkin Street Youth Services

The enduring strength of Larkin Street's soul over its 28-year history has resulted principally from three key phenomena. First, the Larkin Street cause of helping homeless youth on San Francisco Streets continues to be compelling—in fact, the problem has grown in severity—over the years. Second, generations of Larkin Street board members, executive directors, and professional staff have never wavered in their beliefs that youth should be saved, are resilient, and should be accepted for care regardless of the complexity of their plight. And the agency's mission remains vital. As a result, the board's culture has been faithfully maintained, and only people with a passion for the organization's mission and a willingness to roll up their sleeves versus just lending their names are invited on to the board. Finally, over time, the Larkin Street board of directors and staff have learned to tell the organization's story and its youths' stories to themselves and to the outside community. From these stories, the Larkin Street community has learned much about the organization's origins, the poignant journeys of the youth whom it has served, the effectiveness of Larkin Street programs in support of youth, the evolving needs of homeless youth, and the deep struggle of all such youths in successfully restarting their lives and leaving the streets for good.

Having deeper and broader understanding has reinforced key beliefs and philosophies about the youth and about Larkin Street's mission and its approaches. This, in turn, has further inspired the board, staff, and volunteers to deepen their commitment to the organization and added to the meaning that stakeholders derive from their contributions and associations with Larkin Street. In recent years, Larkin Street's story has been retold principally through a lovingly created written history, *Larkin Street Youth Services: The First 25 Years*, a volume that was painstakingly compiled and written by a founding and long-serving volunteer and board member, Bill Campbell, on the occasion of the agency's twenty-fifth anniversary. The stories are also told through the agency's occasional reports on youth homelessness and its work.

Board members, staff members, and volunteers attend ceremonies and celebrations to mark important milestones in Larkin Street youths' journeys away from the streets (such as high school graduations and job-readiness-course graduation ceremonies). These occasions are touching reminders of the youths' needs, their resilience, and the organization's fine work. Larkin Street's stories are also generated by volunteers who mentor individual youth, staff members who work one-on-one with youth, and volunteers who serve holiday meals to groups of Larkin Street youth or who go out on to the streets where homeless youth congregate to tell them about the availability of Larkin Street programs and resources.

Dodge & Cox

Dodge & Cox sustains its strong and stable 80-plus-year soul by keeping alive its founders' core beliefs, philosophies, and learning, which, as you will remember, include a commitment to financial conservatism, a long-term investment perspective, and perceptions that banks and brokerage firms were not generally aligned with clients. You might also recall that the firm's founders undertook a 15-year effort to launch the investment management firm during the Great Depression and World War II. Dodge & Cox's soul was also nourished by the successful and satisfying partnerships formed during those highly challenging, foundation-building decades, as well as by the organization's high-minded desire to "bring the force of some order into a rather chaotic investment world."[6]

The firm's evolving financial success in the 1950s and 1960s validated its conservative, long-term, value-oriented investment thesis and reinforced the core beliefs, values, and practices on which the firm was built: Do the right thing for clients,[7] remain independent and privately owned, utilize a multi-person and cautious long-term investment decision process, and share the firm's financial success with employees. In the 1980s, 1990s, and 2000s, various management practices and decisions continued to solidify, reinforce, and reflect the firm's essence. One of these decisions was to keep the firm relatively small and housed in a single office suite to facilitate easy interactions among staff. In addition, leaders avoided outside ownership of the firm in

[6] E. Morris Cox and Lawton Kennedy, "*Dodge & Cox: The First Fifty Years.*"

[7] A senior employee spoke about his early years with the firm: "Mr. Dodge and Mr. Cox always used to lecture us, 'Be sure you emphasize the clients you have. Don't worry about getting new ones. If you do a good job with the ones you have, you'll get new ones.'"

order to maintain its independence in investment decision-making and its overall alignment with clients' interests. Employees were not rewarded for asset gathering or sales activities, so their attention remained on investment analysis and decision-making. As related in 2011 by Gregory Serrurier, vice president and portfolio manager, "There remains no one who is compensated based on new business, no culture that stops client work based on account size or even measures the size of the business in each relationship, any more than existed when I arrived in 1984."

Dodge & Cox also offered only a few investment products so as to guard against the dilution of the staff's attention on existing clients and investment decisions. They honored a teamwork approach in order to obtain many individuals' ideas and views on investment decisions. Titles were not generally used in an effort to support collegiality. "Stars" were not tolerated or rewarded, nor were individuals who acted aggressively for their own self-promotion. Rather, working with collegiality and consensus was the preferred ambiance. The company believed in paying individuals well and regarded long-term contribution to the firm an important indicator of performance. No quantitative measurements were made of how well individuals' stock recommendations performed because so many persons were involved in each investment decision, they were considered the *firm's* ideas.

Of vital importance in promulgating Dodge & Cox's soul over the years has been its practice of hiring most investment personnel directly from school and shaping their mindset over the years as employees. Also important are the long careers[8] that most employees have at Dodge & Cox (30-plus years in many instances). There were three generations of long-serving leaders: Misters Dodge and Cox for almost 40 years; Peter Avenali, who was hired in 1946 and became co-leader with Joe Fee for about 35 years; and Harry Hagey, who joined the firm in 1967 and co-led it from the late 1980s to 2006 with John Gunn, who had joined the company in 1972. The model of shared responsibility in leadership fit well and contributed significantly to the firm's culture and management practices. This model continues today with the co-CEO titles used by Dana Emery and Charles Pohl.

During Hagey's long tenure as CEO, in his words, he led the firm from his heart and considered employees to be family. He had much concern for the firm's well-being, served as its rudder, and exuded tremendous pride in Dodge & Cox. Under Hagey's leadership and inspiration, the firm's executives shared many lunchtime conversations about Dodge & Cox's values and what the firm

---

[8] For example, Dodge & Cox's international stock fund is managed by the firm's nine-person investment policy committee. Five of these individuals have worked at Dodge & Cox for 23–39 years, and the other four for 11–16 years; the average committee member's tenure is 21 years.

stood for. New employees, who were often top graduates from leading universities, were educated by the CEO and by other executives on what was important to the firm.

As a well-liked and charismatic leader, Hagey circulated through the firm frequently, informally encouraging individuals and groups to work according to the firm's values and always to act ethically. In Hagey's words, "I walked around a lot and checked in with employees. If individuals ever acted disrespectfully to others, I asked them to desist—speaking with love and acting fairly. Sometimes I read the letters from clients who thanked us for our manner, concern, and dedication. I often reminded colleagues how important our work was to our clients, comparing us to a fiduciary—we have been entrusted with safekeeping others' assets. I viewed myself as the 'keeper of the culture.' I cared about, respected, and loved the individuals who worked at Dodge & Cox, and wanted to know what was going on in their private lives."

Within the parameters of cautious conservatism, the firm did make occasional large adjustments to its strategy in response to changing market circumstances. In 1960, for example, the firm decided to focus on institutional[9] investment managers in addition to traditional individual account management. In the mid-1980s, in response to the growth of the defined contribution business, Dodge & Cox registered to do business in all 50 states, not just in a few Western states. In early 2002, the firm began an international stock fund in recognition of the growing importance of being global. By 2008, the firm established a global stock fund, which reflected the evolution of its investment thinking.

Stanford University

In carrying out Stanford University's quest for excellence in all that it undertakes and in order to foster the pioneering, creative, and entrepreneurial spirit that are core elements of its soul, Stanford has deliberately sought to bring together great people of different disciplines so that they may inspire each other. Importantly, this desire was prompted by the recognition that society's and science's challenges require the collaborative efforts of researchers from multiple disciplines.[10] Thus, Stanford invests in highly attractive on-campus housing, spaces, and facilities for faculty and graduate students so that intellectuals from different disciplines can collaborate, more readily pursue their academic interests on campus, and work in comfortable physical proximity to one another. Stanford has also taken great care to plan

---

[9] By 2011, approximately 90 percent of the firm's business is serving institutional clients.

[10] Stanford *2002 Annual Report*, p. 6.

a serene and beautiful physical environment on its more than 8,000-acre campus to support individuals' happiness, serenity, and work.

Stanford's president manages a discretionary fund to foster interdisciplinary work involving biology, engineering, medicine, and other fields and to fuel pioneering explorations and new idea generation. And, on a related note, the university has long-standing close and mutually beneficial relationships with nearby Silicon Valley biotech and high-tech industries. Finally, the university continues to invest in, encourage, and support outstanding athletic programs to draw together the diverse populations on the campus through common interest, pride, and inspiration.

The Stanford founders' vision, hopes, values, and ideals are frequently and widely referred to and retold for the benefit of its students, alumni, and faculty by its presidents and deans in university histories and feature articles. The well-managed and well-resourced alumni association actively supports alumni reunions and alumni gatherings in major cities around the world. At these occasions, as well as during fundraising periods, the Stanford legacy is retold and proud updates about the university are shared.

Barclay's Global Investors

Barclay's Global Investors' soul remained very strong for over 40 years (through 2009, when it was acquired by Black Rock), principally for four reasons. First, BGI had a very strong, companywide belief that its role and destiny was to make the world a better place. Excerpts from the firm's vision and mission statements reflect such principles:

> Our conviction is that scientific investing provides the most effective way for our clients and people who depend on investment success to meet their financial goals. ... Because of what we do ... more people retire securely, governments manage public assets more effectively, colleges and universities fund more scholarships and research, and charities and foundations better meet the needs of their beneficiaries.

Second, BGI was committed to hiring very smart, well-educated, hardworking finance employees who thrived on intellectual interactions with one another and were fascinated with their colleagues' intellects. The firm also specifically looked for applicants who possessed a strong sense of intellectual elitism, took great pride in colleagues' and their own credentials and accomplishments, constantly pushed toward the intellectual frontiers of portfolio management and its real-world applications, gained the market's respect and mandates versus traditional investment managers, and had confidence that BGI could become known as the most advanced, capable, investment manager on the planet.

Third, BGI's soul was able to stay strong for more than four decades thanks to the leadership of its two highly respected and adored leaders: Fred Grauer and, following him, Pattie Dunn. Grauer, who was an exceedingly smart and avant-garde investment and capital markets thinker, recruited many other top thinkers like himself, maintained relationships with world-class academicians and finance theorists, and built the fast-growing firm from a few dozen employees when he took over to more than 800 employees whom he considered "had suitable fire in their belly." For her part, Dunn, who became co-CEO with Grauer and then succeeded him, had matured with the firm in marketing, sales, and administrative positions. As CEO, she spoke often at BGI gatherings about what made BGI different, why employees should feel proud of what they were creating and achieving, and why they should all continue to pursue what they were proud of.

To nurture BGI's continued zeal and best practices and to set its course for the future, Grauer, Dunn, and another senior BGI executive, Garrett Bouton, created forums and workshops that brought together the firm's top 150 leaders globally. In groups of 20, these senior-level individuals worked through how the organization should be managed to pursue industry leadership as it continued to grow rapidly. They also explored how the firm should stoke its fire-in-the-belly spirit and how it could best coalesce behind its high-minded aspirations to "create financial freedom and security for millions of individuals and thousands of organizations around the world."

Finally, the fourth reason why BGI was able to maintain such a strong soul for so long was due, according to Bouton, to the collaborative establishment of four shared corporate values—trust, knowledge, creativity, and passion—all of which significantly helped to define and reinforce BGI's organizational culture.

San Francisco International Airport

SFO's soul has remained strong over recent decades for five principal reasons. First and foremost, SFO benefits from the continuity it has achieved; the long tenure of senior-level executives and much of the 1,500-person airport commission staff has provided consistency in important areas. As a result, SFO's many years of living according to its desired behaviors and values have ingrained them into the organization. Second, the leadership style of SFO's airport director, John Martin, is to engage with employees everywhere in

SFO[11] and to recognize individuals for their efforts, achievements, and length of service. In other words, Martin's leadership has benefited the airport with his excellent communication skills. Martin delivers periodic "State of the Airport" addresses to assembled[12] SFO employees and writes a weekly blog to keep the airport commission staff informed about SFO's plans, priorities, achievements, and awards. Martin explained, "We can't use money to motivate, recognize, or reward staff. Instead, we want our employees to feel *part* of the organization, *pride* in it, feel *fairly* treated, and *recognized* when they go above assigned duties."

Third, SFO's soul has been strengthened by its mission focus: As a public sector enterprise, SFO is, by its very nature, a mission-driven service organization. The airport also sets and meets high standards, an achievement that serves as the fourth reason why its soul is so strong. The airport director and the deputy directors continuously aim for the highest-possible SFO performance, as demonstrated by a sample of objectives from the airport's 2011–2016 strategic plan:

- Be ranked #1 by passengers in customer satisfaction as a U.S. international gateway airport by two industry-specific surveys;

- Be the airport of choice for premium passengers;

- Be ranked one of the Bay Area's best employers;

- Be among the first airports to achieve carbon neutrality by 2012.

Finally, the fifth reason why SFO has been able to maintain the integrity of its soul is because the organization lives by its values and delivers on its high aspirations. As examples, SFO continually seeks to employ state-of-the-art technology in its operations to ensure maximum safety and security. It maintains an extensive art collection and aviation museum in beautifully designed terminals to create the highest possible levels of customer satisfaction.[13] SFO also has a very high level of diversity among its employees

---

[11] The SFO director walks around the airport daily, observing its myriad operations and speaking with employees.

[12] Director Martin gives the address to all three shifts (including at 4 a.m.) because SFO is always staffed 24/7.

[13] Remodeled Terminal 2, opened in April 2011 at a cost of $388 million, is airy, naturally lit, and boasts many interesting, attractive, and bold works of art, cozy armchairs, 350 power outlets for electronic gadgets, a "recomposure zone" with cushioned ottomans for travelers after security checks, a sleek wood-paneled lobby, a food hall modeled after the one in San Francisco's Ferry Building with some of the same upscale Bay Area restaurants, and live musical performances. SFO is the only U.S. airport that has an accredited museum. In Terminal 2, music is played in security checkpoints to create a calming effect. Chloe Veltman,

(as of March 2011, 30 percent of employees were white, 13 percent Hispanic, 15 percent Filipino, 8 percent African-American, 34 percent Asian or Pacific Islander, and 0.21 percent Native American), and employees feel respected regardless of race, gender, or ethnicity. Because of SFO's committed follow-through on its high aims, SFO's aspirations and beliefs are recognized, respected, and reinforced among employees.

All of the 11 organizations highlighted in this book share several important explanations of why their souls have remained strong over their long lives.

All have compelling causes that are associated with the problems of society and/or a group of people in need that the organization's members consider important. Furthermore, these causes are high-minded, virtuous, inspiring, and galvanizing within the organizations (such as the cry of the poor, homeless youth, bringing order to a chaotic world, bringing financial security to millions, helping owners, helping mainstream investors build and protect their wealth, and so on).

All consider themselves to be in service to others.

All are proud of their organizations, their colleagues, and themselves.

All believe their organization is unique.

All derive inspiration, meaning, principles, role models, and pride from their founders, their organization's founding stories, and/or the examples set by certain organizational leaders.

All draw strength from the respect and validation of those whom they serve, including their clients, larger communities, marketplaces, and stakeholders.

All have organizational cultures that demonstrate ample respect, caring, appreciation, and support for individuals, and all are characterized by trust, candor, and a family feeling.

All consider it vitally important to nourish, preserve, and strengthen the various elements of their souls. They use stories[14] about their organization in

---

"Airport Art Is Not an Oxymoron, At Least Not at SFO," *New York Times*, April 1, 2011; Ben Mutzabaugh, "San Francisco Airport's New Terminal 2 Dazzles," *USA Today*, April 12, 2011.

[14] "We create ourselves out of the stories we tell about our lives, stories that impose purpose and meaning on experiences that often seem random and discontinuous. As we scrutinize our own past in the effort to explain ourselves to ourselves, we discover—or invent—consistent motivations, characteristic patterns, fundamental values, a sense of self." Drew Gilpin Faust, "Living History," *Harvard Magazine* (May–June 2003): 39–43, 81–83. "Stories shape the way we learn how to approach the world. If the stories speak to the struggles and hopes of our own experience, they give us confidence in our future." Alan Briskin, *The Stirring of the Soul in the Workplace* (Bessett-Koehler Publishers, Inc., 1998, p. xvii).

forums and town hall meetings. They widely distribute these stories in thought papers,[15] booklets, reports, and their websites. They place value in historical artifacts and icons.[16] They hold training seminars and off-sites[17] to educate, elevate, inspire, and remind themselves of their important beliefs, principles, and causes. They focus on the benefits they provide to others, and they are constantly seeking to define what constitutes exemplary behavior and success.[18] Through these processes, employees develop an awareness of what unites them. Their hope for the future is strengthened, and they attain a greater sense of connection to each other and to their organization's history.

All of these organizations have relatively long-serving members and leaders who are able to consistently carry and model their organization's important messages, spirit, stories, and values to newer generations of employees. These individuals are also willing and able to mentor and train newer employees.

Finally, all have leaders who embody their organizations' souls. What these leaders care about, what they speak about, how they seek to energize and support their organizations, and how they endorse and reinforce the various elements of their organizations' souls in their decisions, policies, and behaviors—all of these behaviors are conducted while keeping at the forefront of their minds the elements of the organization's soul.

HP was regarded as a "good story-telling company … the yarns, passed on from employee to employee, were mostly about Bill and Dave … and their no-nonsense down-to-earth management style and well-known concern for employees. Others tell of how this style defined the company's culture of openness and innovations, belovedly known as the 'HP Way.'" Benjamin Pimentes, "The Story on HP," *San Francisco Chronicle* October 6, 2002, pp. 61, 68.

[15] Jack Welch, the highly regarded GE CEO, reputedly developed annually a 20-page explanation of GE's vision and values that was shared and discussed with all business teams.

[16] The symbolic and galvanizing importance given to the Wells Fargo stagecoach, Merrill Lynch bull, and SFO International Terminal and T-2 all bear a striking similarity to the power of a nation's flag. "I remember long moments staring at it [the Stars and Stripes] wondering to myself how a piece of cloth could have such power." Jacob Needleman, *The American Soul* (2002, p. 33).

[17] "Taking an interest in one's own soul requires a certain amount of space for *reflection* and *appreciation*." Thomas Moore, *Care of the Soul* (1992, p. 14).

[18] A simple but powerful example of an organization's approach to reminding its members and recruits about success is offered by the U.S. Navy SEALS. After an individual graduates from the arduous and lengthy entry-level "Buds" training and tests, he or she is allowed to wear a brown T-shirt, whereas "Buds" participants wear white T-shirts.

CHAPTER 6

What Can Weaken or Destroy Organizations' Souls

The immediate aftermath of the sudden, surprising, and somewhat mysterious departure of Mark Hurd as Hewlett-Packard's CEO in August 2010 included press allegations of how unpopular Hurd had been among longtime HP employees and executives. The *New York Times* reported that Hurd had "systematically destroy[ed] what had always made HP great ... [by] 'chopping R. & D.,' which had always been sacred at HP." The article also discussed "Mr. Hurd's dictum that HP executives resign from all civic boards, as well as his decision to cut off many of HP's philanthropic activities." "HP had always been a model corporate citizen," said Charlie House, a former longtime HP engineer. Plus, he continued, "Mr. Hurd was incredibly rude and demeaning, and relied on the fear factor ... He was wrecking our image, personally demeaning us, and chopping our future."[1]

---

1 "Real Reason for Ousting HP's Chief," *New York Times*, August 13, 2010, p. B1.

As noted earlier, Hewlett-Packard had long been viewed as one of America's most remarkable companies,[2] built on the aspirations, values, and philosophies of its founders Bill Hewlett and David Packard. With only an outsider's awareness of HP, one can conjecture that the cited employees' backlash to Hurd was because Hurd had, in effect, attacked HP's soul. In other words, he had contravened the company's founding legacy, its spirit of product innovation, its "advancements of science, industry, and human welfare," its egalitarian spirit. Also clearly compromised were the trust, respect, and support of HP employees;[3] the company's long-time policy of sharing business upsides and downsides with its employees; HP's corporate integrity; and its serious sense of responsibility to society, including its corporate philanthropy.

Beyond the specific truths of Hurd's departure and the related HP employees' response, the example raises the important broader questions of what can threaten an organization's soul, and how can an organization counter such threats? The examples that follow focus on these questions.

Williams-Sonoma

In the case of Williams-Sonoma, a threat to its soul arose years ago, when it was in a rapid growth phase. Company leaders determined that the organization needed additional "professionalization" of certain management practices. Departing from its custom of promoting from within, two high-level executives were recruited from the outside: one who was well versed in management control practices and the other who was an expert in human resources management. The two new executives did not seek to learn about the company's culture or traditions, nor did they request counsel from existing employees or build relationships with them. When newly introduced cost control, cost cutting, and inventory management were rolled out, and many new senior-level managers were hired, the associates' fears grew that the company's warm family feeling, traditions, promotions from within, and spirit of collaboration would be lost, along with many of their jobs.

As the operating intentions and approaches adopted by these new executives and their impact on the organization became clearer and more worrisome, legacy company management "reclaimed" leadership of those functions, "took

---

[2] In its first 50 years, HP grew nearly 20 percent a year without a loss. "Architects of the Info Age," *Business Week*, March 29, 2004, p. 22.

[3] Indeed, in 1957, Hewlett and Packard conducted a management off-site "to craft a kind of corporate constitution ... that included an insistence on making techno-contributions while also providing a 'sense of satisfaction and accomplishment' for employees working with 'great freedom of action.'" David Jacobson, "Founding Fathers," *Stanford Magazine*, July/August 1998, p. 62.

back the culture," and reverted to following loyally the company's historic beliefs and values. They sought other ways to "professionalize" its management that were aligned with its core beliefs and spirit and thus avoided significant lasting damage to its soul. In the years since, Williams-Sonoma Inc. has been able to continue to build upon its marketplace strengths, find new ways to serve its customers while increasing its profit margins, and develop a formidable and rapidly growing online direct-to-customer business channel. The company also has launched the West Elm brand, expanded into select foreign markets, and increased the company's market share.

Merrill Lynch

The threats to Merrill Lynch's soul also partly stemmed from changing business circumstances and the impact of new "outsider" leadership. In the 1980s, the firm, whose roots were in retail private client brokerage, began to build an investment banking and capital markets business to remain competitive with other large Wall Street firms and to preserve its independence. Merrill Lynch acquired new wholesale businesses, which were operated by bankers and traders recruited from other investment banking firms. They arrived at Merrill Lynch as carriers of various other organizations' cultures, mentalities, and work practices. Mother Merrill had little to no meaning or relevance to them.

Over the ensuing 10 to 15 years, despite occasional efforts to imbue into the new investment bankers and traders the traditional Merrill Lynch brokerage culture and values, Merrill Lynch became increasingly fractionalized. Its wholesale and retail businesses had little to do with each other, were populated by different kinds of employees, and each had its own culture and affiliations. The traditional Merrill Lynch's soul was thus alive, nourished, and important only in the brokerage part of the firm.

In the late 1990s when Merrill Lynch experienced deteriorating profit margins and return on equity, its board of directors selected a new leader, Stan O'Neal, who was a 15-year veteran of the firm's wholesale business. O'Neal, selected over two longtime Merrill Lynch private client/brokerage leaders, had not grown up with the Mother Merrill private client business history, ambiance, values, spirit, or family feeling. Indeed, as was recounted in a 2001 *Wall Street Journal* article, O'Neal's views of Mother Merrill were not positive or respectful. O'Neal was quoted as saying, "I think that this is a great firm, but greatness is not an entitlement … There are some things about our culture I do not want to change ... But I don't like maternalism or paternalism in a corporate setting, as the name 'Mother Merrill' implies."[4]

In the words of a former corporate officer, "Stan O'Neal viewed Mother Merrill as an object to *kill*. It signified an 'old boys' network.' It didn't judge individuals by accountability for performance. Stan thought there was too much dead wood; there were not enough women or African-American employees because of the old boys' network; gays could not come out. We were Irish Catholic, white, from the same schools. There were too many yes-men." As described by the former head of a Merrill Lynch private client business unit: "When O'Neal became president of the entire private client business, he made us feel beneath him, not important in the grand scheme of the company, and [he] believed that we were paid too much. He made it seem that what we did was low class. In all of his communications to the client advisors, he showed no understanding of what we did."

While serving as president of Merrill Lynch and then as the firm's CEO, O'Neal brought in many new leaders for the private client business who had not worked in that line of business before (some were from capital markets backgrounds and, notably, James Gorman[5] had been a McKinsey consultant) and who had not grown up in the Mother Merrill culture or at Merrill Lynch. O'Neal kept the "old guard" private client/brokerage leaders from influencing key decisions about the private client business; oversaw the release of approximately 15,000 employees (including many longtime "culture carriers"); and repudiated Charlie Merrill's principles. He also stopped further development of a comprehensive history of Merrill Lynch that had been underway, and "squeezed out" (in the words of a longtime Merrill Lynch employee) an attractive and popular Merrill Lynch museum in the main lobby of the firm's New York world headquarters that portrayed the time lines of Merrill Lynch's evolution and displayed many of its old photographs. During this era of large-scale layoffs and the attempted destruction of the soul of Merrill Lynch's private client business, thousands of employees and alumni who shared the Merrill Lynch soul grieved for their individual and collective losses and were angry with O'Neal and his lieutenants.

When Merrill Lynch was acquired by Bank of America, "We feared that the brand and culture would be destroyed, and we sensed the death of Merrill Lynch," explained one employee. Indeed, in the early stages of the Bank of America's integration of Merrill Lynch, it appeared that what remained of

---

[4] Charles Gasparino, "Bull by the Horns," *Wall Street Journal*, November 2, 2011. Also discussed in Andrew Ross Sorkin, *Too Big to Fail* (New York: Viking Penguin, 2009), pp. 141–147.

[5] CEO of Morgan Stanley at time of publication.

Merrill Lynch's soul would be altogether lost—or at least tremendously diluted. But, over time, Bank of America executives decided to leave Merrill Lynch alone—especially the global wealth management unit (the higher-end private client business), which was considered by many to be Merrill Lynch's crown jewel. Bank of America permitted Merrill Lynch legacy employees to consider themselves part of Merrill Lynch (not Bank of America Merrill Lynch), maintain their Merrill Lynch cultural ties, retain Merrill Lynch e-mail addresses, and include the Merrill Lynch bull logo on their business cards (in all other parts of the organization, the identity is Bank of America Merrill Lynch). The logo represents the long-held values and principles of Merrill Lynch.

In the words of another Merrill Lynch private client business unit executive, "Today (June 2010), Merrill Lynch's soul exists in Merrill Lynch employees who remain at Bank of America. The bank let us continue how we used to be, and most of our unit's Merrill Lynch leadership and employees are still here. We keep Charlie Merrill's principles displayed on our walls, and our name is 'Merrill Lynch.'" In the words of a 37-year Merrill Lynch Midwest office manager: "We are now rebuilding our culture. Our office still believes in and feels like Merrill Lynch. The bull has come back in all of our advertisements. We are keeping our identity and growing with it."

Levi Strauss & Company

Over its nearly 160-year history, Levi Strauss & Company had many struggles for its economic survival, notably after the 1906 San Francisco earthquake; during the Great Depression; in the early 1980s, when blue denim was widely available and competition grew dramatically; and while the company's international business was not profitable. On each such occasion, the continuity in the founding family's leadership and its unswerving commitment to its core values precluded any erosion in the organization's soul.

Other potential challenges to Levi Strauss & Company's soul occurred during various periods of rapid growth when large numbers of new employees were hired. The company was challenged to on-board them effectively so that it could learn and benefit from their new ideas. Concurrently, the company had to ensure that new employees could learn and adopt the proud history, special meanings, and core values of Levi Strauss & Company.

In the early 1980s, during very difficult economic times, the CEO convened the senior leadership to reexamine what the company stood for and what made it special. Many years later, when business was weak, some critics believed that so much focus on values was a waste of management's time and was a distraction from commercial challenges. It wasn't sufficiently clear to critics how the company's values were tied to the commercial aspects of the business. Thus, in the early 2000s, the CEO (the first of three non-family members to lead the company) also convened the global leadership to discuss extensively what was special about the company and how its values were connected to the business. The ensuing discussion, which was grounded in Levi Strauss & Company's rich history and its real-life examples, ultimately produced a series of core explanations of the important relationship between values and business results—an explanation created for the benefit of employees that remains unchanged today.

Levi Strauss & Company, with its long history that dates back to the California Gold Rush, was able to maintain and evolve the elements of its rich soul largely as the result of continuity in its (familial) leadership's beliefs and philosophies over the generations. The highly respectable nature of its quest, beliefs, and philosophies in the eyes of its workforce and communities also plays a role, as does the engagement of its employees in periodic assessments of the elements of its soul (although *soul* was likely not the term used in such discussions). Finally, the retelling of its corporate stories about its founding, struggles in the early years, proud history of its jeans, and what Levi Strauss and the evolving company believed in and how it acted on its beliefs—often as a pioneer—also serve to solidify and preserve its soul.

Dodge & Cox

Dodge & Cox has experienced several types of threats to its soul. First, as new types of significant business opportunities arose, the firm's management had to wrestle with trade-offs associated with pursuing new opportunities while attempting to retain its historic approaches. As an example, the long-term growth in mutual funds as investment vehicles and their huge size as asset pools provided significant asset-gathering opportunities and financial success for the firm. In so doing, however, mutual funds threatened two core Dodge & Cox philosophies: its commitment to providing a quality approach to individual clients and its dedication to maintaining Dodge & Cox independent control over investment decisions. After much executive deliberation about the myriad implications of building the mutual fund business during a period of tremendous growth, in 2004 the firm decided to close the Dodge & Cox Stock and Balance funds to new investors in order to best serve current clients. This action reaffirmed the firm's commitment to high-quality investment management over asset gathering, when pursuing both was inconsistent with the firm's beliefs. (When market growth slowed in 2008, the funds were reopened.)

Another threat Dodge & Cox faced was, that as the firm grew, it had several opportunities to go public or to be acquired by larger investment managers.

Both options offered considerable financial rewards to Dodge & Cox employees, but both also transgressed the firm's core principles. After much deliberation, the firm's leaders chose to remain independent and privately owned. "We did not want pressure put on us to earn more money or to dictate how we ran the firm," explained a former CEO.

The dot-com boom proved yet another test for Dodge & Cox. Despite the fact that all of its competitors were diving into the market during this time, the firm decided, after considerable discussion, to desist from investing heavily in technology stocks because their high price/earnings multiples did not fit Dodge & Cox's investment criteria. As tech stocks and the S&P 500 Index (a Dodge & Cox benchmark) soared, the firm's portfolio returns lagged the S&P 500 and competitors' investment performances. As a result, some clients lost faith in Dodge & Cox, thinking the firm was not with the times, and a few separate account clients withdrew their funds. Management continued to reaffirm and reinforce the long-standing investment philosophy and principles, however, which quelled much of the nervousness and self-doubt among Dodge & Cox employees.[6] A few years later, when the dot-com bubble burst and technology and most stocks declined sharply, Dodge & Cox delivered very positive returns, far ahead of the market.

Another challenge to the firm's soul came from certain recent hires from leading MBA programs, whose career hopes, personal ambitions, aggressive personalities, and/or impatience with some of the firm's slow and inclusive decision processes did not comfortably align with Dodge & Cox philosophies, beliefs, practices, and culture. After noting and then evaluating how to deal with these challenges, the firm's leadership reaffirmed its rationale for recruiting top graduates from leading business schools. At the same time, however, it also highlighted the suitability of its flat organizational structure and its slow, inclusive, and deliberative investments processes; its "no stars" beliefs; and the appropriateness for compensation purposes of taking a long-term/team-oriented view of individuals' contribution to the firm. Over the years, a few dissatisfied individuals left as management continued to reaffirm the long-standing elements in Dodge & Cox's soul. Others "made their peace" and remained with the firm, moderating their behavior and awaiting opportunities to influence the firm's future choices while operating within the firm's ethos.

---

[6] A senior Dodge & Cox professional explained, "It is really hard to recreate in 2011 how much pressure there was, because the whole world was so certain that the Internet was the most incredible investment opportunity of all time and valuation didn't matter. We're in Silicon Valley, so at backyard barbecues, cocktail parties, and soccer games, we were being questioned all the time: 'when are you guys going to get with the program?!'"

Dodge & Cox has nourished its soul over the firm's approximately 75-year evolution (which has included several kinds of threats to both the firm and to the various elements of its soul) principally through the impressive longevity of its leaders and long tenure of many members of its workforce, all of whom strongly implanted into the organization what was considered important and right. The commercial success and many satisfactions employees experienced over the years, both of which are believed to be associated with elements in the firm's soul (although it is doubtful that the term *soul* was used by employees when describing what was important to their firm or why they succeeded), also served to strengthen and solidify the firm's soul. Finally, the very conservative and thoughtful nature of the firm's decision-making about embracing change played a key role as well.

Sisters of Mercy

The soul of the Sisters of Mercy has often been challenged by the complexities involved in adapting to changing times and circumstances. The organization requires of its members an exceptional commitment to selfless and lifetime service to the poor and the courageous will to take on the toughest of challenges. These requirements set a high bar for each new generation of prospective members. As described by two Sisters of Mercy, Sister Mary Ann Scofield and Sister Marilyn Lacey, the following situations are illustrative of these types of challenges to the organization's soul.

"Over the past 50 years," Sister Marilyn explains, "we Mercys have initiated substantial change in both our internal structures and our external presence in the world in order to facilitate our mission in a rapidly changing world. In fact, Catherine McAuley, our foundress, never wanted to start a religious order. She and a colleague simply began doing good works among the poor in Dublin. In the early 1800s, however," Sister Marilyn continues, "it was scandalous for unmarried women to be out on their own, serving the poor in slums and living together for mutual support and common prayer. The Vatican intervened, threatening to shut down these innovative women of mercy unless they became a 'legitimate' community of nuns under the authority of the Church. Reluctantly, [Catherine] agreed [to form an order of nuns]— solely so that the mission could continue. She subjected herself and her followers to the nineteenth-century rules of religious orders, to the vows, the habit, the enclosure (semi-cloister), and the daily schedule of prayers. The new community then functioned under the authority of local bishops, with whom Catherine had many an argument in her day."

Sister Marilyn next discusses a second situation that tried the Sisters of Mercy's soul. "When the Catholic Church's renewal movement of the 1960s encouraged religious women to return to their founding spirit, the Sisters of Mercy began to shed many historical accretions. Some changes were internal and not noticeable to the general public (our governance changed from top-down, unquestioning obedience to a more communal style of decision-making). Other changes were immediately visible and controversial among Catholics—putting aside our medieval habit in favor of contemporary dress, for example, or moving out of traditional school and hospital settings into a wide variety of other ministries." She continues, "Always the challenge has been to maintain the charism while adapting the lifestyle and works."

Sister Mary Ann notes that the heart of the Mercy vocation is the call from God, a call that must be tended like a small inner flame, lest it be smothered by the clamor of other demands: "We Sisters are immersed in the culture of *overwork* that permeates America. Our mission is vital and paramount, but it flows only from our relationship with God, which must—like any relationship—be nurtured. We are constantly challenged," Sister Mary Ann continues, "to make time for prayer, solitude, and retreats, to find the right balance between contemplation and work, so that our presence in the world is never merely the 'busyness' of good works but always the joy that witnesses to the fact that God is more than enough."

"All of our ministries began with efforts to be with the poor," says Sister Marilyn. "Over decades and centuries, however, populations who were once poor moved up from poverty into the middle class. Mercy moved with them! Hospitals that initially served desperately poor immigrants, for example, evolved into multi-million-dollar institutions. We Sisters, then, face an ongoing dilemma: How do we choose, again and again, to stay true to our mission?" Sister Marilyn continues, "One way is to make certain that even our grandest institutions—our universities, healthcare systems, schools, etc.—always provide significant outreach and services (usually uncompensated) for the very poor. Another is to use this institutional base and success to connect the resources of the wealthy with the needs of the poor, facilitating the interface between those disparate worlds. A third way is to encourage and support individual Sisters who initiate new works among the poor (such as the work of Catherine's Center, a safe house in the San Francisco Bay Area for women coming out of prison, or the work of Mercy Beyond Borders, which partners with displaced women living in extreme poverty overseas). And finally," she concludes, "all of us Sisters engage in advocacy, using our geographic coverage, our influence, and our relationships to educate and advocate for systemic changes that 'make right' the terrible imbalances in the world that keep the poor oppressed."

Sister Mary Ann comments on the fact that the number of Sisters has dropped off sharply in recent decades: "The abrupt 'reduction in force' facing most religious communities in Europe and America today, including Mercy, probably stems from two dramatic cultural shifts: (1) Families tend now to have only one or two children; and (2) lifelong commitments are relatively rare. When Catholic families routinely had numerous children," she explains, "it was common for at least one to join a convent or seminary. That is not the demographic we see today. And in today's culture of instant gratification and constant change, making lifelong vows of poverty, celibacy, and obedience is certainly countercultural—if not perceived as downright bizarre. For these reasons, and perhaps many others," Sister Mary Ann continues, "fewer and fewer women are choosing to enter religious communities in the twenty-first century. Only time will tell what this portends for the future of the Sisters of Mercy worldwide."

Wells Fargo Bank

The principal challenges to Wells Fargo's soul have arisen when its vision and values and/or business model have been called into question by critics and various senior officers and directors who wondered if they were still valid. Recently, such questioning arose in association with the bank's stance regarding subprime residential lending and investment banking. Other important banks, such as Countrywide, that traditionally were important residential mortgage competitors of Wells Fargo took significant market share from Wells Fargo when Wells refrained from aggressively engaging in subprime lending. Amid the questioning of many about Wells's self-imposed restraint, CEO Richard Kovacevich explained, "Subprime contravened our vision and values; we refused to permit the bank to engage in many of the subprime industry practices (that could have made the company money in the short-term, but were not in the customers' best interest)." Notwithstanding this explanation, he continued, "When our results were not nearly as good as competitors', and we lost many of our good commission salespeople to competitors, critics picked on our culture, assumptions, and business model. We were called 'old fashioned,' 'in denial,' not part of 'the new world,' etc. I refused to bend," Kovacevich explained, "and made certain that everyone in the bank knew my reasoning. A firm's soul and culture have to be embraced by *all* of its employees, whenever business is done, and senior leadership must *continue* to act in alignment with the vision and values during a crisis. Acting true to our soul," he concluded, "embeds it all the more in the hearts and minds of our employees forever. And, in the aftermath of the 2008–2009 financial crisis, Wells Fargo subprime decisions have been vindicated."

"Another example is investment banking," Kovacevich said. "We did *not* acquire a big investment bank during the 1990s and early 2000s, as other large commercial banks did, because the cultures of investment banks, with their emphases on large transactions and 'star' players, were incompatible with our culture. We predicted that most of those acquisitions would fail, and," he continued, "most of them did. When we acquired Wachovia, we did increase our investment banking activities. Because the financial crisis led to the demise of many investment banks and has dramatically changed the industry, Wells Fargo can offer traditional banking services without compromising our ethics, our culture, or our vision and values." He concluded, "We are pleased that we waited for things to change." And pleased he should be. As of May 25, 2012, Wells Fargo was first in market value and fourth in total assets among its U.S. peer group of large national banks and financial services companies.

Stanford University

Stanford University's soul has been challenged over the years by the great earthquakes of 1906 and 1989, the Great Depression, and the financial market crash in 2008–2009. Each of these external events put significant pressure on the university's financial resources and its economic well-being, which in turn threatened its ability to pursue the highest levels of intellectual and athletic excellence, pioneering, innovation, and entrepreneurship. In these dramatic instances, Stanford's leadership made adjustments to its financial forecasts and management and renewed efforts to fund-raise, but the university did not compromise any of its core principles and quests. In the words of one of the university's senior staff: "It is a key characteristic of elite research universities to always move forward—no matter what the challenges."

The longstanding quest for excellence and the highest possible academic and athletic performance challenges Stanford to avoid being seduced into an "arms race" with other great universities for exceptional faculty, students, and athletes. To counter this temptation, the university routinely avoids placing its focus on winning the competition, instead opting to pursue the highest standards. A final risk to Stanford's soul is that its ample resources could induce a sense of being too comfortable and self-satisfied with its contemporary approaches and achievements—and thereby detract from its entrepreneurial and innovative spirit.

University of Notre Dame

The challenges to Notre Dame's soul over the years relate principally to the complexities of being a Catholic institution with a long tradition of seeking meaningful engagement with the wider society while remaining open to challenges and the big issues of the day. In recent times, a high-profile example of such a challenge was the invitation issued by Notre Dame's president, the

Rev. John I. Jenkins, C.S.C., to U.S. President Barack Obama to receive an honorary degree and to serve as the commencement speaker at Notre Dame's 2009 graduation ceremony. The invitation sparked strenuous opposition from some segments of Notre Dame's alumni, faculty, and students who found great dissatisfaction with certain policies and beliefs held by President Obama. In the face of a demanding confrontation, Jenkins did not back off but explained: "Because Notre Dame stands for something, complex issues become intensified. In response to the complexities, as president, I take the pulpit and talk to the various audiences about who we are, what we stand for, and why we do what we do. My intent is to clarify and to deepen commitment."

San Francisco International Airport

Periodically, SFO has had to deal with significant external shocks that could have threatened its economic or operational viability; employees' confidence, commitment, or morale; and even the airport's soul. In the eyes of Director John Martin, the most notable shocks the airport has faced were 9/11; the United Airlines' bankruptcy (SFO is a United hub), when SFO lost 35 percent of its traffic and some of its workforce; and the 2008–2010 severe economic turndown, when the San Francisco government's fiscal challenges brought frozen salaries, mandatory furlough days, and the possibility of layoffs. "In all of these difficult times," Martin explained, "we really stepped up, and the outside forces were not a threat. We modified our operating plans and priorities; we maintained communications with everyone in the organization; we continued to be mission-driven; we aimed high in all that we did; and we recognized employees who went beyond their assigned duties (e.g., helped lost or stranded passengers, came up with great new ideas, and/or picked up trash). Everyone understood the need to do more with fewer resources," Martin continued. "We also helped everyone feel a part of SFO and kept up everyone's pride in the airport. We made sure that none of these threats affected employees' commitment or the organization's soul."

"What sometimes did challenge SFO's soul," explained Martin, "were individual employees who acted on the job as independent agents or who had their own goals that were not aligned with what's best for the airport. We want employees who will put SFO's overall interests above their own and their unit's interests. We will not accept such behaviors, and we work hard to gain everyone's support for SFO's objectives," he concluded.

As an overview of why SFO's soul has survived and flourished over many years, the discussion above and in early chapters highlight the contributions of strong, trusted, highly respected, and continuing leadership by airport Director

John Martin; long-tenured employees throughout the organization; and employees' great pride in SFO and their desires to see it rise to world-class recognition while continuing their employment at the airport. Thus, the elements of soul that have contributed to SFO's success and achievements have been implanted over time by leadership strength and continuity among the entire SFO community and then reinforced by employees' long-term orientation to SFO careers and the airport's ongoing recognition and achievements.

The preceding examples about what can challenge an organization's soul emphasize the importance of leadership. A change in leaders and/or leadership mindset can threaten or weaken an organization's soul if the new leader deliberately seeks to destroy elements of its soul (for example, Stan O'Neal of Merrill Lynch); acts insensitively to its soul (such as Williams-Sonoma's newly recruited executives); or contravenes elements of its soul (examples include Mark Hurd at HP, and Gil Amelio at Apple, who, after Steve Jobs's departure, sought to diminish the company's various founding quests, commitments, beliefs, and philosophies and instead principally emphasized making money).

When an organization is acquired by, or merged with, another organization, the inherent risks to its soul are evident. But, in the two cases cited, Bank of America ultimately showed respect for Merrill Lynch's wealth management business and encouraged elements of its soul to thrive; and the "new" Wells Fargo deliberately merged key elements of the two legacy banks' souls and emerged even stronger.

As the preceding company examples also make clear, another threat to an organization's soul can arise when an organization's employee population changes significantly. When new recruits don't have an awareness, affinity, or emotional commitment to their organization's soul and/or, if new employees have not been involved in building their organization's soul (such as when Merrill Lynch acquired/hired investment bankers from other firms), the elements of its soul can become diluted in their importance and influence in the organization. Levi Strauss & Company recognized this risk when it hired large numbers of employees, which is why the company deliberately sent them to cultural orientation sessions. SFO has a similar philosophy in place in that the airport will not accept employees who place their *own* interests or their unit's interests above the airport's interests.

The demands of changing times, to which each organization must determine how best to adapt, are also an ongoing threat to any organization's soul. The changes after Vatican II posed a risk to the Sisters of Mercy. Fast-growing Williams-Sonoma's determination in the 1990s to professionalize its executive ranks with outside hires easily could have crippled the company's soul.

Similarly, Dodge & Cox's investment philosophy vis-à-vis technology stocks was questioned during the dot-com boom, as was Wells Fargo's decision to refrain from subprime lending in the run-up to the bursting of the housing bubble. Finally, Merrill Lynch's strategic determination to build investment banking alongside its long-standing private client/brokerage business most certainly tested its soul. Despite the many tough decisions these organizations were forced to make in order to keep up with changing times, they consistently sought to stay true to the things that had always seen them through in the past—the principal elements of their souls.

A final, indirect threat to any organization's soul could arise if storytelling and other information exchanges by employees who share and honor their organization's history, core beliefs and philosophies, and accomplishments are curtailed. Benign neglect, leaders' lack of respect or appreciation for the importance of such exchanges, cost cutting, deliberate attempts to destroy the soul, and/or acquisitions and mergers—any and all of these situational circumstances could silence employee storytelling. Apparent in the foregoing examples is that an organization's soul can be both vulnerable and resilient. As is true with all human systems and organizations, the soul requires nourishment to thrive.

To conclude this chapter—and to highlight the importance of staying true to one's soul—let's look at what can happen when an organization strays from its soul. Arthur Andersen LLP, once the world's largest professional services firm with more than $9 billion revenues and 85,000 employees in 2001, serves as a dramatic example. Begun in 1913, Arthur Andersen grew to become one of the country's most reputable auditors. Its soul was comprised principally of the conservative founder's motto, "Think Straight, Talk Straight," and his four cornerstones, which were intended to guide employees' behavior. These cornerstones included providing good service to the client, producing quality audits, managing staff well, and producing profits for the firm. Its reputation as an auditor and employer was that of integrity and high values.

After the founder's death in 1947, however, a series of business-related strategic, leadership, and cultural choices gradually moved the firm away from its soul. First, in 1950, Arthur Andersen formed a technology consulting practice that grew rapidly and ultimately became larger and more profitable than its auditing business. The firm's consultants had a different mentality from its auditors; were much more growth-, sales-, and money-driven; and developed notably larger and more lucrative business opportunities. Then, in the late 1960s, the firm stopped requiring all partners to work for two years in Audit. Future Andersen consultants, therefore, lacked a cultural bond with Audit and its values. Next, in the late 1980s, Andersen auditors were instructed to engage in selling activities, with much of their performance evaluation and compensation determined by how much new business they brought in. Allegedly, this pressure ultimately caused at least some of the auditors to be less stringent and demanding with their audit clients. The 1990s brought about attempts to save money, and as a result, many of the firm's auditors were forced to retire at 56, thus reducing the corps of experienced and senior-level culture carriers and the availability of seasoned auditors to lead the firm's audit assignments. After 1996, the new worldwide head of auditing exhorted auditors to cross-sell extra services to their audit clients, an imperative that he summarized in his "2x" strategy: Partners should bring in two times their revenues in work outside their area of practice. Ultimately, the firm encountered serious quality issues with many of its audits, had to pay several very large fines levied by regulatory agencies, and collapsed in 2002 with the Enron indictment. In summary, over time Arthur Andersen's four cornerstones were trivialized to three pebbles and a boulder. Making profits was what really mattered.[7]

---

[7] This account is based on Ken Brown and Ianthe Jeanne Dugan, "Andersen's Fall from Grace Is a Tale of Greed and Miscues," *Wall Street Journal*, June 6, 2002; and A. Neela Radhika, *The Fall of Arthur Andersen* (Hyderabad, India: Center for Management Research, 2003).

Finding, Reviving, and Recreating Lost Souls

Recently, senior partners of a rapidly growing information security consulting firm decided to find and build on the soul of their firm as part of an intended renewal of its culture and strategy. The creation of the firm was the amalgamated result of a "roll up" of nine formerly independent partnerships in the same type of business that came together in the late 1990's dot-com boom. Through 2011, the nine smaller firms had been permitted to continue working in their legacy professional practice groupings, to keep their existing clients, and to pursue new client relationships as they did in the days when they functioned as independent partnerships.

The senior partners were mindful and somewhat concerned that their firm did not have a cohesive sense of identity. While there existed many fond and proud remembrances of the individual consulting partnerships' respective foundings, struggles to grow, admirable leaders, business successes, and business principles, in 2012 there was very little sense of shared history, culture, or identity. Aside from various companywide administrative policies and processes, including its compensation program and bonus pool, the most important commonalities across the firm in 2012 were an evolved set of understandings about how the firm should relate to its clients, that were large financial services firms and large retail businesses. These understandings, which had contributed to successful revenue production, included the following:

- Roll up our sleeves and work alongside the client;
- Do whatever it takes to get the work done right;
- Understand the client's business model and what the client is trying to do;
- Focus on solving the client's problem rather than selling it more services;
- Understand how to work with the client's team;
- Have integrity and tell the truth—even if it is bad news.

Widespread respect for these principles existed within the firm, and its employees took pride in the fact that they followed the principles. These principles had not evolved collaboratively or deliberately through cross-firm discussions; rather, they reflected the respective legacy partnerships' acquired wisdom over the years about business development and client relationships.

Given the well-publicized and sophisticated security breaches and cyber attacks on corporate America and the U.S. government, new information security firms were being formed weekly to meet the growing demand for risk assessment and protection. Thus, in 2012, the firm's senior partners sensed that their organization needed to renew and strengthen its spirit, identity, cohesiveness, brand, strategy, and various management practices in order to attract quality professionals and to avoid losing its employees to start-up competition. In both a strategic and emotional sense, professionals across the firm needed satisfying answers to the question: why does it make more sense to remain part of a large firm that is comprised of nine smaller ones than it does to return to the earlier model of operating as small, close-knit partnerships with ample opportunities to grow?

Since organizational strategy and vision per se are not the focus of this book, we will leave aside discussions regarding the firm's economic rationale for its decision to pave a strategic and aspirational path into the future. What is relevant here is that the senior partners came to recognize that finding the firm's soul was critically important for holding it together, for breathing fresh spirit, inspiration, and meaning into the 600-employee-strong organization, and for galvanizing the employees. The senior partners came to believe that the process of finding and reviving its soul would create the bedrock upon which a vibrant, twenty-first century firm could flourish.

How should this information security consulting firm (and other organizations like it) go about finding its soul? A three-step process is recommended:

1. **Discover it:** To do so, examine and draw from the organization's heritage, legacy, and its founding history; and catalogue the passions, values, beliefs, and philosophies of current employees;

2. **Bring it to life:** Articulate the soul for the entire organization;

3. **Embed it:** Put in place processes and practices that will keep the soul alive and robust.

In more specific terms, here is how the firm might proceed. The five elements of soul, which were described in Chapter 4, provide the framework. Organizations can ask themselves five questions:

1. What are our principal concerns about people or clients who need help and which of their problem(s) should be solved?

2. What is our organization's principal quest, and how will we commit ourselves to addressing our concerns and providing our services to the people we are concerned about?

3. What are our collective understandings and wisdom about how best to successfully address our concerns noted above? (Note: the firm's shared principles for business development and partnering with clients cited earlier in this chapter are key answers to this question.)

4. What are our core philosophies and beliefs about how we conduct our work and operate as an organization of people? What behaviors will be appropriate when we relate to each other as employee colleagues, as service providers to our clients, and as we undertake our work?

5. What stories about our various founders, leaders, and influential employees inspire us today, and resonate strongly? Set the bar for us? And, point the way?

In order to initiate the firm's soul discovery process, its senior partners could engage a sizeable number of employees across the firm at all levels to explore in facilitated small group discussions their remembrances, sentiments, ideas, views, and passion about what means the most to them about the firm's purpose—and why. These employees could also explore:

- What kind of mark the firm should leave on its industry, marketplace, and communities—and why;

- What kind of reputation the firm should have in the eyes of prospective clients, current clients, prospective employees, and current employees—and why;

- What it should feel like to work for the firm —and why;

- What stories resonate and are the most inspirational about the firm's past, its past and current leaders and other employees—and why.

Subsequently, all employees who participate in these small group discussions can be invited to a second round of facilitated discussions, where they are assigned to small groups with entirely different participants. The small groups can be given the output from the first round of discussions, and this information can be arrayed and organized as "answers" to the five soul questions presented above. The groups could be asked to clarify, explain, embellish, exemplify, and reaffirm the respective answers, after which they could be encouraged to assess the relative importance of the content in each answer. Subsequently, a cross-firm senior management group could review the output from the two rounds of small group discussions and recommend what should be regarded as the five principal ingredients of the organization's soul.

In this recommended soul-finding process, many employees will have participated, thus contributing what is important to them from the heritage and legacies of the nine former IT security consulting firms that comprise the current organization. Through such participation, genuine voice will have been given to all participants. The process of remixing the small group composition will add further clarity and evaluation of what is most important to the overall employee population. The two sets of small group participation will also help all participants develop common understandings about the questions discussed, which will help to build a coherent, one-firm organization. The inclusive process will also help convince participants that the final definition of the firm's soul meaningfully reflects the organization. All participants can thus feel ownership, pride, and alignment with the soul.

Once the organization's soul has been defined, the next important process is to make it feel real, meaningful, satisfying, and inspirational for the organization. Drawing on the experiences cited in Chapter 3 of organizations whose souls have remained vital over long periods of time, several important process principles can serve as guides.

First, the elements of an organization's soul need to be presented, aired, explored, and used as reminders of what is most important to the members of the organization. Doing so will help to spread the power of the soul as a source of guidance and inspiration and can help to "weave together the past, present, and future."[1] Recall that Sisters of Mercy "matriculate" through years of such exploration upon joining the organization. Later they are reminded of their organization's soul and can raise questions about it with their mentors and at retreats. Levi Strauss & Company's periodic employee meetings revisit such questions as, "What is important to us?" and "Why are we different?"—that are helpful in reclarifying its rich soul. At Stanford, the president's speeches and columns in university publications remind students, faculty, staff, and alumni about Leland and Jane Stanford's 1890s vision for the university. At Notre Dame, the president periodically uses the powers of his office and his platform to provoke, explain, and remind the university community what Notre Dame stands for as a Catholic institution of higher education. This communications strategy proves especially important when the university embraces the many conflicts and challenges facing American society. In Notre Dame's classrooms, social gatherings, faculty meetings, student clubs, and so on, the explorations and debates can then be unleashed and expanded.

At Wells Fargo, the periodic publication of the bank's "Vision and Values" booklet is accompanied by numerous employee-attended town hall meetings in which questions and dilemmas pertaining to living by the organization's espoused principles can be raised. This practice helps to clarify what counts the most to the bank and how its core beliefs and philosophies should be embodied throughout the organization. The leadership team at Barclays Global Investors, in partnership with all of the firm's managing directors, devoted more than one week to a forum exploring the firm's core, its future, and its leadership requirements. For years, Johnson & Johnson's CEO hosted CREDO Challenge Forums to bring together managers from around the world to discuss, explore, and evaluate the company's Credo to determine if it remained relevant, required revisions, or should be discarded. At Williams-Sonoma, asking "What would Chuck do?" and posting Howard's Rules serve as frequent reminders of the key leaders' vision and approaches.

Second, the use of stories about the organization's founding, pivotal moments in its evolution, its leaders' vision and principles, its icons, and its values are all vitally important reminders of the other elements of its soul. Stories also connect current employees to the organization's past. As referenced in Chapter 1, Hewlett-Packard was a storytelling company, with the focus often placed on the founders Hewlett and Packard, and the Palo Alto garage in which the company was formed was revered as an important icon. Wells Fargo's stagecoach is a widely used and cherished icon. There are dozens of stories of Nordstrom employees' extraordinary service to customers. In Levi Strauss & Company's head office, the company's museum is an inviting and endearing visual reminder of its past and its association with the American

---

[1] Lee Bolman and Terrence Deal, *Leading with Soul* (Jossey-Bass, 2001, p. 148).

West. Larkin Street tells stories of the youth it serves (without identifying the specific youth by name) to remind the public, volunteers, its board of directors, and its employees of not only youths' challenges but also the support they receive from the organization. Its proud history is also captured in a book about its first 25 years. Sisters of Mercy shares stories about its founder's devotion and her deeds on behalf of the poor. The organization also highlights courageous and dedicated sisters of the past and present. Merrill Lynch's private client employees loved to gather for training, conferences, and special events and share stories about the humble origins and career progressions of the firm's various CEOs. They also respectfully recalled founder Charlie Merrill's early principles and his dedication to clients.

Third, the many businesses and not-for-profits cited in this book have found ways to honor the work of their organizations, the units within them, and the individuals whose attitudes, efforts, and/or achievements are admirable reflections of what the organization deems most important. Indeed, SFO presents two such airport-wide employee annual awards, and Williams-Sonoma gives three. Merrill Lynch had annual conferences for outstanding achievers. Larkin Street has an annual Paving the Way Gala at which the organization celebrates client youths' progress and achievements and honors the work of its staff and volunteers. Stanford and Notre Dame's graduation ceremonies honor and celebrate academia's and the universities' traditions and values; their alumni associations honor volunteers; and both universities honor scholarship and academic achievements in various ways. In 2011, SFO had a huge celebration for the community to mark the re-opening of its beautiful, state-of-the-art, environmentally green Terminal 2, as well as a celebratory open house for staff and their families.

In these ways, organizations can explain, clarify, honor, glorify, elevate, emphasize, and remind employees of their most important meanings, the sources of their vitality, their essential character, and their transcendent ideals. In other words, they define anew and celebrate their souls.

To make the soul real and maximally powerful, however, it must be lived in the daily decisions, priorities, initiatives, and activities of the entire organization. The elements of an organization's soul must also be referenced often by the leaders in their explanations of the choices they make. Thus, the president of Notre Dame, Rev. John I. Jenkins, C.S.C., "stood tall" when many of his constituents opposed his decision to invite U.S. President Barack Obama to serve as the university's 2009 commencement speaker and to receive an honorary degree. Jenkins also explained the relevant ideals that guided his decision. Wells Fargo CEO Richard Kovacevich refused to permit the bank to engage in subprime lending because it would not have been in customers' best interests and thereby contravened the bank's "Vision and Values" statement.

SFO will not condone managers who place their own unit's interests ahead of the entire airport's well-being. And Dodge & Cox refrained from selling itself for a considerable sum to avoid losing its independence in investment decisions.

CHAPTER 8

Young Organizations' Souls

Young organizations normally have exceptionally dynamic, demanding, and fragile existences. Their strategic path can be off the mark, and they must endure zigs and zags in strategy as new insights about challenges and opportunities arise. Their financial base is often difficult to secure and subject to uncertainties and changes in funders' support. Their efforts to gain traction in a desired marketplace or domain usually involve an uphill competitive struggle. Their progress is likely to look much different from what they and their backers had originally anticipated it would. Furthermore, because of the limits imposed on young organizations by thin staffing, if key employees leave, they can experience great stress and organizational dysfunction in their efforts to cover the human-resource gaps. Recruiting the right employees can be slow. Hiring mistakes can be made, resulting in potential setbacks. Understandings about goals, priorities, and desired approaches can evolve unaligned among the leadership group. The IT and administrative infrastructures are likely to be underdeveloped and only partially reliable. The list of potential pitfalls and vulnerabilities young organizations face goes on and on. Suffice it to say that operating in a young organization is tough work with highly unknowable future prospects.

The early histories of the eleven organizations[1] featured in this book reveal that these organizations were not exempt from the many struggles that today's young organizations face. For example, in the 1850s, eight newly arrived Sisters of Mercy and separately a young man named Levi Strauss had to establish themselves in the rough-and-tumble Gold Rush Era of young San Francisco, while Wells Fargo stagecoaches had to safely and successfully cross the rugged West. Dodge & Cox had to build their firm during the Great Depression and World War II. Chuck Williams's four kitchen stores were a failing business until Howard Lester bought them. Larkin Street's board of directors had to make a crucial decision early in the agency's existence: should the organization continue to serve only as a drop-in center that provided emergency shelter to disadvantaged youth and refer them to city agencies for their other needs? Or, should Larkin Street's services be expanded to meet a broader range of youths' immediate and longer-term needs with the more ambitious goal of helping them exit the streets for good? Merrill Lynch built a brokerage business with lower-economic-class immigrants and first-generation Americans. Stanford University had to attract quality faculty to a new university in the then-distant and little-known state of California. Earlier, Holy Cross priests from France had to travel to the United States, where they founded the University of Notre Dame in rural Indiana, far from major urban centers.

Among the many struggles involved in growing a young organization, one of the most important leadership challenges is building a motivated, well-functioning, aligned, productive, and turned-on workforce. The particular challenges of doing so in a young organization are numerous. New employees may not receive sufficient on-boarding that aligns them with the organization's core raison d'être, goals, strategies, priorities, values, and codes of conduct. People working in young organizations can burn out from overstimulation, hard work, and the requirement to continuously meet new challenges and adapt to ever-changing circumstances. Similarly, the employees can get lost in the specifics of managing and responding to the ongoing changes their young organization undergoes. They can become demoralized by the unending challenges and/or setbacks their organization experiences. Their roles and the rules of engagement when interacting with their counterparts within the organization may not be well defined or understood by all who should be aware. Senior management may make decisions that are not transparent or understandable to the employees. Employees' needs for coaching and for clarifications about their roles and/or objectives can be overlooked or undermanaged by their busy bosses.

---

[1] Another prominent organization, Bank of America, which was begun in the early 1900s in a one-room office in San Francisco's International Quarter, had to survive the great earthquake and fire of 1906, business panic, and war in its first 10–15 years.

Because young organizations must confront a magnitude of dynamic and demanding challenges such as those cited above, people working in young organizations need certain forms of support to help them through their ongoing challenges:

- Reinforcement of the organization's purpose so their motivation and commitment remain high;

- Sources of stability that offer them continued confidence in the future and help them retain the ability to focus on the work to be done;

- Common understandings and reference points to facilitate communications, collaboration, and alignment among employees;

- Confidence in their organization's purpose, leadership, strategic journey, approaches, capabilities, ability to get the job done, and resilience when mistakes and setbacks occur;

- Confidence in themselves so that they can focus on the work to be done, use initiative when appropriate, and maintain their commitment, energy, and satisfaction;

- Ways of working together that are responsive to the organization's tasks, dynamics, and newness;

- Ways to get their individual needs met so morale, satisfaction, and commitment can be maintained.

These needs and organizational requirements can be met in part by the process recommended in this chapter for developing a young organization's soul and also by the resulting soul itself. The recommended soul-searching process consists of engaging many or all of the young organization's employees in a round of facilitated, small-group discussions about the five principal elements in an organization's soul:

1. The concerns that the organization has about certain people who need help and/or certain problems in society that should be solved;

2. The organization's principal quest and commitment to addressing its concerns;

3. The organization's collective wisdom and understandings about how it can address its concerns;

4. The organization's philosophies and beliefs about what is important, what counts the most, what should constitute success and satisfaction, and what behaviors are appropriate when employees relate to each other, clients, and their work;

5. The stories about the young organization's founding, founders, leaders, and select employees that inspire, set the bar, and point the way for others.

The founder(s) and visionary(ies) of a young organization searching for its soul might lead the initial discussions among employees about the first four soul elements. These leaders might also provide explanations and answers to their colleagues' questions regarding the creation of the young organization's soul. In any subsequent discussions about these four elements of soul, it might be beneficial if they are led by others in the organization who possess functional expertise and have responsibility related to each of the four soul elements. For example, the third soul element, the organization's wisdom and understandings about how to address its concerns, might be discussed by those who best know the organization's strategy, technology, resource deployment, administrative processes, service delivery, intellectual property, and/or other sources of competitive advantage. The organization's principal quest and commitment to addressing its concerns, soul element # 2, might be best discussed by those most connected to formulating the organization's objectives, purposes, and strategy.

Consideration of soul element #4, the organization's philosophies and beliefs, could be done in multiple small discussion groups in which participants are asked to propose and discuss organizational values, desired behaviors, operating principles, and the rules of engagement among employees. After employees voice their ideas, suggestions, and responses to others' ideas, the organization's leader(s) can integrate and then finalize the choices of philosophies and beliefs that should underlie its culture and management practices. Similarly, founders and founding stories, which make up soul element #5, could be addressed in facilitated discussions among employees in which stories, principles, and achievements that resonate most among the employees (and why) are surfaced. These discussions could also incorporate employees' thoughts on how best to retell the organization's stories in the future at employee gatherings, when recruiting new employees, and when on-boarding new recruits.

Overall, the organization's leader(s) can bring together, reevaluate, integrate, refine, and finalize the results of the employees' ideas and discussions about the five soul elements. The organization's soul can then be presented back to the entire organization for its edification, questions, and confirmation. Specific follow-up tasks can be assigned to various employees to implement the spirit of the soul in tangible terms and to create alignment with the soul.

An important byproduct of the recommended soul-searching process is that it will address many of the young organization's core needs, which were enumerated earlier in this chapter. Stability and confidence will come from added clarity and conviction about the organization's aspirations, capabilities, resources, cohesion, demonstrated ability to work together, and the qualities of its leadership and resources. Ways of working together and ways for individuals to get their needs met will derive from codifying organizational philosophies and beliefs to include values, rules of engagement, and codes of conduct. Common understandings and reference points will result from extensive discussions and explorations about the desired elements of the organization's soul. Finally, clarification of organizational purpose will arise throughout employee discussions regarding their concerns and their collective determination to do something about their concerns.

Over time, leaders can bring together their colleagues at all levels to review and possibly refresh the components of their organization's soul so as to be inspired and grounded by the process of sharing high-level meanings, aspirations, and determinations. Leaders can also periodically question how each element of their organization's soul applies to contemporary realities and explore possible modifications to the soul. Doing so will ensure that the soul can continue to live and that its vibrancy and relevance are maintained. At organizational forums, leaders and select employees can share stories that ably reflect and enrich the organization's soul, as Merrill Lynch brokerage employees and Williams-Sonoma associates have done with so much enthusiasm and meaning at their conferences and training sessions.

An example of a young company that perceived it could potentially derive benefits from developing its soul is Rodan + Fields Dermatologists, a company built around the professional dreams, reputations, and persona of two Stanford-trained dermatologists, Katie Rodan and Kathy Fields. More than a decade prior to launching Rodan + Fields Dermatologists, the doctors formulated an over-the-counter acne regimen known as Proactiv. The product was then marketed nationally on a 30-minute infomercial, which featured explanations from the doctors as to how and why their new approach to treating acne worked and highlighted testimonials from successfully treated customers. Proactiv's sales grew rapidly. Today in 2012, millions of customers around the world are satisfied users of the three-step system, and the product continues to have one of the highest grossing revenues in infomercial history.

The two doctors next set their sights on the rapidly growing $2.5 billion U.S. anti-aging skincare market. In 2002, they founded Rodan + Fields Dermatologists as a prestige skincare retail brand, and their business strategy was based on their proven model of combining over-the-counter medications with elegant skincare in a multistep regimen. From decades of practicing dermatology, the doctors had witnessed how closely self-esteem is linked to healthy skin. Because one's face is a biological "calling card" to others, a clear, youthful-looking complexion can make a real difference in peoples' lives. As a result, belief that their unique approach would produce visible benefits to skin without a prescription or visit to a dermatologist formed the basis for their creation of their new and sustainable brand. More precisely, the Rodan + Fields Dermatologists brand targeted a multitude of common skin problems related to aging, with specific regimens for sun damage, wrinkles, and facial redness. Depending on the issue of greatest concern, a customer would select one 60-day-dose regimen containing three or four Rodan + Fields products. Deliberate daily care at home would result in a noticeable improvement without the need for a visit to a dermatologist, injections, or invasive procedures. Each customer would become a walking advertisement for the brand.

Initially, Rodan + Fields's products were sold in high-end department stores through the Estée Lauder Company, which acquired the brand in 2003. Although the brand had limited distribution, the products were top sellers in the clinical skincare category. Gradually, however, the doctors and their business partner, Ammon Rodan,[2] came to recognize that much of the demand for their products resulted from highly satisfied users influencing their friends, family members, and colleagues to try the products. Traditional high-end retail distribution and salesclerks were not the key for creating demand for these new products. Instead, what Rodan + Fields Dermatologists needed was a national "army" of passionate and knowledgeable product advocates who believed in the products, could seek out prospective buyers, provide considerable direct contact with these prospects using compelling education, and offer follow-up service to them. Ultimately, Doctors Rodan and Fields bought back their brand from Estée Lauder, repositioned and retrofitted the brand and their business model, and relaunched Rodan + Fields Dermatologists in 2008 as a direct-selling business through network marketing.

The basic ingredients of the brand's current business approach are fourfold:

1. Development of skincare regimens each targeted for a specific dermatologic issue with products that combine over-the-counter medicines with cosmetic ingredients. Each step in a regimen builds on the next and guarantees to improve the quality and appearance of one's skin within 60 days.

---

[2] Katie's husband

2. Direct person-to-person sales of the products by thousands of Rodan + Fields advocates (called "consultants") who, as independent business operators, are trained, supported, and compensated by the company.

3. Doctors Rodan and Fields reinforce and leverage their authority as skincare experts to give both consultants and customers confidence and trust in their products. With the publication of their book *Write Your Skin a Prescription for Change*, through their frequent interviews with the beauty press, and in communications via social media, the doctors maintain their credibility and relevance for the goodwill of their brand.

4. The sales efforts of Rodan + Fields consultants are supported by a steady stream of customer testimonials, independent clinical trials demonstrating product efficacy, and doctor-developed educational materials. Consultants are further motivated to exponentially grow their businesses through an attractive compensation arrangement. This arrangement allows them to earn commissions in two ways: first, on products they sell; and second, on sales by other consultants whom they recruit to the Rodan + Fields organization. Along with financial rewards, public recognition is a key motivator driving the success of Rodan + Fields consultants. At periodic regional and national company conferences, individuals are singled out for awards recognizing their achievements as business leaders. These award ceremonies provide a platform for successful consultants to share their personal stories of triumph over adversity, thereby inspiring other consultants in attendance. The consultants enjoy camaraderie, affinity, and identity as Rodan + Fields consultants and relish the chance to meet the founding doctors. It makes sense, then, that an almost missionary zeal pervades the consultants and company employees, who are moved by the organization's mantra, "Changing skin and changing lives." (The users' lives are changed from healthier skin and the consultants' lives are changed when they became economically freer through their Rodan + Fields earnings.)

To help ground the young, aspirational, energetic, and evolving organization, a mission statement was drafted and distributed to all employees, and a policies-and-procedures manual was developed and provided to each consultant with the understanding that it must be followed. In addition, a leadership advisory group of 12 leading Rodan + Fields consultants was created to provide a feedback loop between the field and headquarters, and a code of ethics was drafted by the leadership advisory group for dissemination to the consultants. Finally, Doctors Rodan and Fields (as founders, icons, and role models) offered a steady stream of personalized testimonials about themselves to reinforce awareness of their dedication to healthy skin and to sharing their business opportunity with the consultants. The doctors espoused, "We will each and all be successful by helping others be successful," and consultants shared with each other various "pinch-me moments" that came from realizing that they could now choose what they wanted to do with their lives, given their Rodan + Fields earning power and economic independence.

The mission statement appears in all Rodan + Field offices and is thought to provide guidance for all decisions:

Rodan + Fields Dermatologists Mission Statement

Our mission is to redefine independent business ownership with brand presence and transformational products to change skin and effective programs to provide income potential to change lives. With integrity beyond reproach, products that exceed our customers' expectations, and commitment to community and marketplace values, we will create an enduring legacy for our Independent Consultants and our employees.

As of May 2011, Rodan + Fields executives were dealing with the challenges of building and supporting a fast-growing consultant corps, hiring numbers of quality staff, upgrading their IT infrastructure to keep pace with the company's rapid growth, and contemplating the complexities of expanding internationally. At that juncture in the company's evolution, with its attractive value proposition for the marketplace leading its growth and development, leaders at Rodan + Fields were considering holding periodic off-sites among a cross section of its management and staff. These off-sites would serve as forums where employees could discuss what the company stood for, the core values that should guide employees' behaviors and decisions, what critical issues needed resolution, what constituted success, and what operating principles and practices best served the organization at work. Other topics that could be discussed included what the organization's ultimate aspirations were and what stories about the company best captured and could convey its essence. Regardless of what specific employee concerns dominated the discussion, however, the end goal was to ensure that there was common understanding and agreement among employees, that the employees had a voice in the company's evolution, and that the organization learned from its experiences and adapted well. Through these periodic discussions, the company would define and help to institutionalize Rodan + Fields's soul.

Rodan + Fields had already coalesced around many of the elements of soul outlined in earlier chapters. Its concerns centered around skin, self-esteem, and financial independence. It was committed to helping enhance customers' self-esteem through skincare products that worked, and its quest was to offer economically attractive opportunities to independent business operators. The company maintained understandings that self-esteem was strongly influenced by appearance and financial independence, and it also knew that what Rodan +Fields offered was best promoted by word of mouth, networks, and the two doctors' reputational authority. It was true to its core beliefs and philosophies about the integrity and transformative potential of both its products and its network-marketing model. Finally, the company cherished founder stories about Doctors Katie Rodan and Kathy Fields as entrepreneurs and visionaries who succeeded with the Proactiv infomercial and continued their legacy through Rodan + Fields Dermatologists.

Author's Note   In September 2011, in Rodan + Fields's San Francisco offices, the company conducted a series of small-group, soul-searching discussion sessions that I facilitated. All of the Rodan + Fields headquarters employees participated in one of the three-hour sessions, each of which was comprised of a mixture of representatives of all grade levels from the company's executive group and all of its departments. Before the discussion sessions, participants were given a written explanation of the soul concept and six questions on which the small groups would be asked to focus. They were also told that the intended purpose of the exercise was to identify the principal elements of Rodan + Fields's soul and assured them that all ideas offered during the discussion sessions would be valued and helpful. Amnon Rodan, the company's chairman, sat in on all of the group sessions, as did a Rodan + Fields staff member who took notes for future review—without attribution.

During the small group discussions, participants demonstrated considerable interest and generated many ideas about the firm's concerns, principal quests and commitments, and its core philosophies and beliefs. They had some difficulty understanding the concept and generating examples of their organization's understandings; and generally only those individuals who had ample contact with customers and consultants were able to generate meaningful stories. Once the stories were told, however, participants readily warmed to them and derived satisfaction and fun from talking about them.

Subsequently, the senior management group reviewed the small discussion groups' output and had several discussions among themselves (some of which I facilitated) to clarify, refine, and amend what the discussion groups had generated. Ultimately, the final version of Rodan + Fields's five elements of soul and the choice of company stories were confirmed by Amnon Rodan and Lori Bush, the company's president. (Bush has years of senior-level management experience at Johnson & Johnson and knows well its Credo and how it was used to guide, inspire, and align employees.) The senior group also discussed how to make the company's soul real and useful in daily Rodan + Fields life, as well as how to roll it out to the entire company. Ultimately, the executives decided to create a video program comprised of representative employees from around the company talking about elements of the soul. The video was then shown at the all-company December holiday party.

Leaving out the Rodan + Fields stories, which are personal, the principal elements of the organization's soul are as follows:

CONCERNS

"We are concerned about people who are seeking a better way to live in their skin. People want purpose. They want to be somebody. They seek self-esteem, independence, and the ability to control their destiny, but they need empowering connections and the support of others who can show them the way."

QUEST & COMMITMENT

"Changing individuals' destinies to empower them to make a difference in the lives of others. Be a clear path and a worthy choice for changing skin and changing lives."

UNDERSTANDINGS

"Great things come from being the best in skincare. Leadership in solving everyday skin concerns is a platform for creating relationships and connections that empower a transformative business opportunity with personal development and recognition, a sense of belonging, and the potential for financial freedom. Because of our great skincare … we are a vehicle to change skin and change lives."

PHILOSOPHIES & BELIEFS

"Love what you do; do it best; do it with passion; do it with integrity; and celebrate how we change our own lives by changing the lives of others. Our power as a team provides us with reason to celebrate."

Hope from Organizations' Souls

Employees and the organizations in which they work are often unaligned in important ways that create tensions, dilemmas, disappointments, and challenges between them. Employees, for their part, often are highly concerned about employment security and receiving sufficient and fair compensation. In addition, they might be worried about not having attractive professional development or advancement opportunities, satisfactory relationships with their bosses and colleagues, or meaningful, interesting, and challenging work. They might not be given suitable recognition and respect by their organization or the freedom to do their jobs as they think appropriate. They might feel out of the know about their organization's overall objectives, strategy, and what their leaders consider most important. We can understand, therefore, why employees might regard their employer with a healthy dose of anxiety, reserve, and mistrust and, as a result, feel an unwillingness or inability to fully engage in their work.

At the same time, leaders of these organizations are generally most concerned about their own objectives, which tend to include growth, meeting their agreed objectives, and charting a future strategic course. They worry about resource sufficiency and allocation and the need to balance different stakeholders' interests. They must respond to threats and crises and seek to leverage their organization's resources and opportunities. Thus, even if leaders and managers genuinely want to address their employees' concerns and hopes, many of them, at all levels in an organization, lack sufficient awareness, sensitivities, know-how, self-confidence, delegated power and freedom to act, and resources to be responsive and to lead and manage effectively.

The associated costs to an organization that lacks alignment between leaders and employees can be large: employees can become disgruntled, frustrated, and under-fulfilled. They can lose their passion, lose hope, disengage, focus on their own well-being rather than the overall organization's objectives, and become dispirited. If many employees respond in this way, overall organizational performance will decline to a level well below its potential.

Improvements to unaligned organizational dynamics and performance results can be slow to occur when incumbent management is stuck in its ways, unaware of employees' problems and dissatisfactions, uncertain of how to deal with employees' concerns, or devoted to a different set of challenges and priorities. Even when new leaders or managers are brought in, time is required for them to assess the problems, determine the best ways to move forward, and implement improvements. For many employees and organizations, then, the workplace environment and organizational performance fall considerably short of aspirations and expectations. Hope for better possibilities has only a weak foundation. As emphasized throughout this book, however, employees and organizations can find the bases for many positive and satisfying results from engaging together—if they find or reclaim the five principal elements of their organization's soul and employ the power of a robust soul for the good of the overall organization.

Table 9-1 is a reminder of the essential elements of an organization's soul and the prospective benefits for the organization that can be associated with each soul element.

Table 9-1. Summary of the Five Elements of Organization Soul and the Associated Benefits for Employees and the Overall Organization

Elements of Soul	Creates ...
Concerns for people and for problems in society to be solved	Shared sense of higher purpose, meaning, pride in organization and self-identification with organization, affinity with other employees, inspiration
Determined quest and commitment to address the organization's concerns	Shared commitment, inspiration, meaning, engagement, identification with organization, pride in organization and self, alignment, goal orientation, affinity with other employees, fulfillment, satisfaction, enjoyment, problem-solving and task-completion mindset
Understandings the organization possesses to help it address its concerns	Greater clarity, common understandings, sense of organizational competence and distinctiveness, pride in organization, higher level of individual and collective performance, less conflict, greater self-confidence and confidence in organization, identification with organization, greater ease in engaging
Philosophies and beliefs about how to operate	Alignment with organization and other employees, sense of affiliation, respect for organization and trust in it, greater ease in working with others, identification with organization, greater commitment to organization and engagement in its workings, less stress, greater sense of empowerment
Stories about organization's origins that highlight its founders, their original mission/purpose, and other employees who were important contributors and role models	Sense of belonging to organization, participating in and contributing to evolving story, clarity about what is important, pride in organization, confidence in organization, identification with organization, inspiration, commitment to organization, affiliation, affinity with other employees, collective and individual courage, alignment

As demonstrated by the many examples shared in this book, a thriving organizational soul can imbue employees with a strong sense of shared purpose and meaning, as well as a personal connection with the organization. It can also serve as a source of inspiration, identity, and pride for employees as they commit to their employer, engage in the work of their organization, and give of themselves to achieve the organization's purpose. Soul also creates a common language for the organization and places the organization's objectives, priorities, and ways of working into a mutually understood framework. It thus creates more focus and clarity about the organization's purpose and direction.

A strong organizational soul can have ample staying power among employees—even if a change in leadership or ownership causes the soul to be subverted or neglected. Earlier in this book, the example of Mark Hurd, Hewlett-Packard's former CEO, was cited, when legacy employees rejected and were angered by Hurd's apparent transgressions of the "HP Way." Likewise, over the years I have met with numerous former Citibankers from the 1970s, 1980s, and 1990s who, in 2012, remained very proud of their former employer when it was arguably one of the world's top two international banks. They still revered the leaders of the day (including Walter Wriston, Thomas Theobald, and George Vojta) and were filled with praiseworthy stories about the leaders and how the institution was built, operated, and succeeded. They could describe with great pride and personal identification the bank's culture, strategies, business practices, and esprit de corps before it became Citigroup in a merger that diminished Citibank's strategic importance and prominence and led to the retirement of thousands of its legacy bankers. The Citibank soul of that earlier era is still very much alive today in the hearts and minds of its veterans, who are now in their sixties and seventies. In fact, in December each year, between 70 and 100 Citibank alumni from that era gather for lunch in New York City to reminisce and commiserate. So, too, are there warm remembrances and bitter memories among former Arthur Andersen partners and employees, who retain their Andersen pride, identity, stories, and beliefs while operating in subcultures of other large employers in which groups of former Andersen employees now work. Similarly, as cited earlier, Merrill Lynch private client employees have kept the Merrill Lynch soul alive within Bank of America—with BoA's permission—despite the traumas of losing thousands of Merrill Lynch employees and then being acquired by Bank of America.

Once strong and vital, an organization's soul can remain alive for a long period of time. But notwithstanding its qualities of endurance, an organization's soul requires nourishment and adaptation to changing times so that its relevance and importance to the organization can continue. A soul is like most other human institutions, conventions, and dynamics: it benefits from use, adaptation to changing times, and investment. The example organizations cited in this book used their souls (even though they did not use the term "soul") repeatedly as guidance for important decisions; sources of inspiration, meaning, and identity for employees; and as a means to anchor the contemporary organization in its historical development, principles, and leader's vision. Consider the example of Stanford University. To keep his organization's soul alive, the university president contributes a column to the periodic alumni magazine in which he explains new university buildings and educational innovations as contemporary expressions of the founders' dreams and aspirations.

When an organization nourishes and makes use of its soul, employees and the employer are rewarded. The processes generate hope among employees by signifying that the organization's future can be made better, by bringing individuals together to explore their common purpose, aspirations, concerns, and possibilities for their future together; and by seeking to evolve or strengthen the soul. In turn, employees' hope for an imagined better future will prompt initiatives that make the aspirations real. These are all positive outcomes.

I wish to conclude with an awareness that is meaningful to me, for it reflects the passion, power, wisdom, and hope that can be associated with an organization's soul. Near the corner of Sutter and Scott Streets in San Francisco is the Women's Health Building of the University of California San Francisco (UCSF). For years, women cancer patients visiting the building for treatment, as well as their caregivers, families, and friends, were given an opportunity to create a ceramic tile on which they could tell their stories and express themselves in words or drawings—each symbolic of a woman's battle with cancer.

The "Tile Project," as it came to be known, was masterminded by two women: Ann Chamberlain, an accomplished artist in works of public art, a Fulbright fellow, and a cancer patient; and Dr. Laura Esserman, the director of the UCSF Breast Care Center, a surgeon and breast cancer specialist. Ultimately, after more than 1,000 women created tiles to share their stories and messages, a 70-foot floor-to-ceiling mosaic of the tiles was created on a wall near the building's entrance that faces the Healing Garden, a quiet place in which patients, caregivers, and staff seek peace and respite. The wall of tiles is similar to the huge AIDS quilts that have been created in remembrance of AIDS victims.

Explained Chamberlain, "In the course of my own treatment for breast cancer, I have been impressed by the network of patients and support groups that bring people together, enabling us to find strength in talking to each other, sharing information and personal experiences. The healing garden and tile wall value the experience of patients and will lend support to others in years to come." Said Dr. Esserman, "You can't walk by without remembering why we are here ... To answer scientific questions, yes. But we are really here to honor these women and their stories, and to dedicate ourselves to bringing hope and better outcomes to all the women who follow."

One tile stands out for me:

Sing every day

Eat chocolate for breakfast

Stand on your head

Sail leaf boats on a river

Live juicy! Tell stories

Eat peaches in the shower with a friend

Laugh a lot, seal your

Fears in an envelope and mail them to Mars

Fill your bathtub with roses

Accept love, paint pictures

Stick out your tongue in the rain, there are no rules!

Kiss a lot

Affirm yourself....

References

Bains, Gurnek, and Kylie Bains. *Meaning Inc.* London: Profile Books, 2007.

Barrett, Richard. "Liberating the Corporate Soul: Building a High-Performance, Values-Driven Organization" (monograph). February 2009.

Bolman, Lee G., and Terrence E. Deal. *Leading with Soul.* San Francisco: Jossey-Bass, 2001.

Briskin, Alan. *The Stirring of Soul in the Workplace.* San Francisco: Berrett-Koehler Publishers, Inc., 1998.

Chalofsky, Neal E. *Meaningful Workplaces.* San Francisco: Jossey-Bass, 2010.

Cohen, Allen, and Clive Matson, eds. *An Eye for an Eye Makes the Whole World Blind: Poets on 9/11.* Oakland: Regent Press, 2002.

Frankl, Viktor E. *Man's Search For Meaning.* New York: Washington Square Press, 1959.

Frattaroli, Elio. *Healing the Soul in the Age of the Brain.* New York: Viking, 2001.

Gardner, John W. *The Tasks of Leadership.* Leadership papers no. 2, "Independent Sector," Washington, D.C., March 1986.

Ghoshal, Sumantra, and Christopher A. Barlett. *The Individualized Corporation.* New York: Harper Business, 1997.

Heilbroner, Robert. *An Inquiry into the Human Prospect.* New York: W.W. Norton & Company, 1974.

Hillman, James. *The Soul's Code: In Search of Character and Calling.* New York: Random House, 1996.

Hodson, Randy. *Dignity at Work.* Cambridge: Cambridge University Press, 2001.

Isaacson, Walter. *Steve Jobs.* New York: Simon & Schuster, 2011.

Klein, Eric, and John Izzo. *Awakening Corporate Soul.* British Columbia, Canada: Fairwinds Press, 1998.

Kotter, John P., and James L. Heskett. *Corporate Culture and Performance.* New York: The Free Press, 1992.

Lama, Dalai, and Howard C. Cutler. *The Art of Happiness.* New York: Riverhead Books, 1998.

Lashinsky, Adam. *Inside Apple.* New York: Business Plus, 2012.

Lerner, Michael. *The Politics of Meaning.* Cambridge, Massachusetts: Perseus Books, 1997.

Maney, Kevin. *The Maverick and His Machine: Thomas Watson, Sr. and the Making of IBM.* Hoboken: Wiley, 2003.

Moore, Thomas. *Care of the Soul.* New York: Harper Collins, 1992.

Needleman, Jacob. *The American Soul.* New York: Jeremy P. Tarcher/ Putnam, 2002.

Packard, David. *The HP Way.* New York: Harper Business, 1995.

Posner, Barry, and Jim Kouzes. *Credibility.* San Francisco: Jossey-Bass, 1993.

Sennett, Richard. *The Corrosion of Character.* New York: W.W. Norton & Company, 1998.

Sorkin, Andrew Ross. *Too Big to Fail.* New York: Viking, 2009.

Ulrich, Dave, and Wendy Ulrich. *The Why of Work.* New York: McGraw Hill, 2010.

Whyte, David. *The Heart Aroused*. New York: Currency Doubleday, 1994.

Wilkins, Alan L. *Developing Corporate Character*. San Francisco: Jossey-Bass, 1989.

Index

CPSIA information can be obtained at www.ICGtesting.com
Printed in the USA
LVOW061146240313

325747LV00003B/400/P